DEAL TERMS

VENTURE CAPITAL DEAL TERMS

A GUIDE TO NEGOTIATING
AND STRUCTURING
VENTURE CAPITAL TRANSACTIONS

HARM F. DE VRIES
MENNO J. VAN LOON
SJOERD MOL

Copyright © 2016

Published by: HMS Media Vof
Authors: Harm F. de Vries, Menno J. van Loon & Sjoerd Mol
Design cover: Gaby de Vries
Design: Haags Bureau
Print: Createspace.com
2nd print: December 2016

www.venturecapitaldealterms.com

ISBN 978-1534663541

No part of this publication may be reproduced by any means, including printing, photocopy, digital files or in any other manner whatsoever, without the prior written permission of the publisher.

While the publisher and authors have used their best efforts in preparing this book, they make no representations or warranties with respect to the accuracy or completeness of the contents of this book and specifically disclaim any implied warranties of merchantability or fitness for a particular purpose. The advice and strategies contained herein may not apply or be suitable for your situation. You should consult with a professional where appropriate.

Neither the authors nor the publisher can be held liable for any actions taken on the part of the reader based on the texts and exercises in this book. The reader shall remain fully liable for any and all such actions.

ABOUT THE AUTHORS

Harm de Vries is co-founder and general partner of several high-tech venture capital funds. Harm has led many investments through different crucial phases, from due diligence to negotiations of terms to growth- and exit phases. Harm serves as a non-executive board member of several portfolio companies. He started his career in 1994 as a lawyer with an international law firm. Harm holds a masters degree in law from the Erasmus University Rotterdam. More information about Harm can be found on www.innovationindustries.com.

Menno van Loon has been working as an interim manager and legal consultant since 2003. Prior to his current professional activities, he worked as an investment banker and lawyer in the U.S. and the Netherlands. Over the past twenty years Menno was involved in venture capital transactions as a lawyer, investment banker and legal consultant, giving him a broad perspective on such transactions. Menno holds a masters degree in law from the University of Groningen.

Sjoerd Mol is an attorney-at-law and partner at Benvalor law firm based in Utrecht, The Netherlands. Sjoerd specialises in mergers & acquisitions and venture capital. His clients include investment funds, business angels and start-ups. Sjoerd is co-founder of www.capitalwaters.nl, an internet platform for early-stage deal documentation, and is active as mentor and legal partner of several start-up accelerator programmes. Sjoerd holds both a masters degree in law and a masters degree in economics from the University of Utrecht.

PREFACE

In 2004, a famous Dutch Professor, whose company we were spinning out of the university, asked me to explain to him exactly what I was asking him to sign. Before him was a term sheet that I had drafted. Because I didn't have a lot of time, I promised him that I would provide him with a written explanation of the most important terms. That's how the idea of writing this book was born. I started writing immediately. However, combining a full-time job with writing a book took more time and effort than I expected, so after five months of scribbling during nights and weekends, I asked my good friend, Menno van Loon, to help me out. Menno and I did the bar exam together, many years before. His experience as a lawyer and later as an investment banker, came in handy. Together we finished the book in twelve months' time and published it with Reed Business Information in 2005, under the title "Venture Capital Term Sheets. How to structure and negotiate venture capital transactions."

Since then a lot has happened. I started new funds and invested in many high-tech companies. The banking crisis came and went and so did many venture firms. Niche law firms emerged, focusing solely on venture transactions. Sjoerd Mol, a partner at one such law firm, suggested to me and Menno that our book was getting outdated and needed adjustment. The three of us set out to update and rewrite the book. We made the book more complete and many of the clauses easier to understand, since we also explained the economics behind the terms. We also added tips and suggestions both for the entrepreneur and the investor. By doing this, we genuinely believe that we have created a level playing field for all stakeholders involved in any venture capital transaction.

For ease of reading we have used male pronouns (he/his/him) throughout the book as a generic pronoun for both genders.

We could not have succeeded in creating this end product without the help of our friends. Also on behalf of Menno and Sjoerd, I would like to especially thank Marlon Dijkshoorn, who helped us with the fine tuning of the financial paragraphs, and Pieter Jan Dorhout, who once again proofread the entire manuscript and changed many phrases into impeccable English. Finally, I would like to thank my sister, Gaby de Vries, for making (again) a beautiful cover for the book.

Harm de Vries

CONTENTS

About the authors		5
Preface		6
1	**Introduction**	11
1.1	Structure of the book	12
1.2	Investment process	12
2	**New wave energy case study**	15
2.1	Incorporation	17
2.2	Seed round	18
2.3	Series A round – early stage phase	19
2.4	Series B round – growth phase	22
2.5	Series C round – further growth	24
2.6	IPO (Initial Public Offering)	26
3	**New wave energy term sheet**	28
4	**Terms explained**	42
4.1	Issuer	42
4.2	Amount of Financing	43
4.3	Milestones	44
4.4	Investors	48
4.5	Type of Security	50
4.6	Warrant Coverage	57
4.7	Share Price and Valuation	59
4.8	Capital Structure	62
4.9	Anticipated Closing Date	63
4.10	Dividends	64
4.11	Redemption	66
4.12	Voluntary Conversion	68
4.13	Automatic Conversion	70
4.14	Anti-Dilution	72
4.15	Pay-to-Play	82
4.16	Liquidation Preference	84
4.17	Favourable Terms	93
4.18	Board Representation	94

4.19	Voting Rights	100
4.20	Consent Rights	101
4.21	Registration Rights	105
4.22	Representations and Warranties	112
4.23	Information Rights	115
4.24	Use of Proceeds	117
4.25	Pre-Emptive Rights	117
4.26	Rights of First Refusal	120
4.27	Co-Sale Right	122
4.28	Drag-Along Right	123
4.29	Management Board	125
4.30	Employee Pool	127
4.31	Vesting Scheme	129
4.32	Founders' Shares	131
4.33	Lock-Up	133
4.34	Employment Relationships	133
4.35	Non-Competition/Non-Solicitation	134
4.36	Non-Disclosure Agreement	135
4.37	Assignment Inventions	137
4.38	Key Man Insurance	138
4.39	Agreements at Closing	139
4.40	Fees and Expenses	140
4.41	Confidentiality	141
4.42	Exclusivity/No-Shop	142
4.43	Governing Law	143
4.44	Non-Binding Character	144
4.45	Indemnities	145
4.46	Conditions Precedent	146
4.47	Expiration	149

Annexes   150

Annex 1: Term sheet template   150
Annex 2: Profit and loss account and cash flow statement case study   175
Annex 3: Glossary of terms   176
Annex 4: IRR Analysis: Years Invested vs. Return Multiple   185

1 INTRODUCTION

Venture capital has established itself as an important source of capital for a variety of companies, ranging from start-ups to more established businesses. Consequently, the number of people who are at some point in their career involved in a venture capital transaction, is steadily increasing. While some people involved in venture capital transactions have extensive experience in this area, the knowledge of others is at best rudimentary. Entrepreneurs in whose company a venture capitalist will invest, lawyers working in this field for the first time, and even junior venture capitalists and angel investors often lack the full understanding of all aspects of venture capital financing required to ensure a successful transaction.

The purpose of this book is to provide a clear understanding of the most frequently used practices, terms and conditions to those with less than extensive experience in venture capital transactions. We believe, however, that this book will also serve as a valuable reference guide for the more experienced venture capitalist.

Practically all venture capital transactions start out with the execution of a term sheet. A term sheet is a document summarising the basic terms and conditions under which investors are prepared to make an investment. It also sets out the structure of the transaction, the parties involved, the timelines for due diligence and the deadline for the closing. A well-drafted term sheet serves as a tool to focus attention of the parties on the essential elements of the investment, and as an instrument to investigate whether there is common ground between the parties regarding the most important investment conditions, before they spend further time, energy and money on negotiating a deal. A term sheet covers the main aspects of a venture capital financing and facilitates the execution of the final transaction documentation.

Effective participation in the negotiations regarding the term sheet is possible only once each party involved fully understands the scope of the terms included in the term sheet (including the commercial implications thereof) and the information it contains, and the alternatives to the terms in use. Moreover, a clear understanding of such terms is likely to expedite the negotiation of the term sheet and completion of the investment process. We hope this book will be of assistance in gaining such an understanding, to the benefit of all parties concerned.

1.1 STRUCTURE OF THE BOOK

This book is intended to be a practical and easy-to-use guide. In section 2 of this chapter, we will first discuss the investment process in general. In chapter 2, a fictional venture capital transaction will be used as the basis for the discussion of the different clauses most commonly used in term sheets. Chapter 3 contains the term sheet that will be submitted to the company trying to raise an investment round in the transaction described in chapter 2. This term sheet will serve as the base for the rest of this book, wherein each subsequent chapter will deal with specific subjects dealt with in the term sheet (e.g. liquidation preference, anti-dilution protection, drag along, and tag along). Each chapter discussing a certain type of clause in the term sheet will include a standard version of such a clause and, if applicable, alternatives to the same, for easy reference. A glossary of terms commonly used in venture capital transactions is attached as Annex 3 of this book.

1.2 INVESTMENT PROCESS

Venture capital firms invest in companies with high growth prospects, enabling them to earn their return upon an *exit* by selling their shareholding of those companies to another company (trade sale) or to the public (in an *initial public offering* or IPO). Venture capital firms usually look to retain their investment for a period of at least three to seven years. This period often depends on the stage the company is in, its growth profile and the opportunity to realise an exit. The stages a venture-backed company will go through in chronological order are generally referred to as the *Seed*, *Early* and *Growth*.

The chance that a company will fail to realise its business plans within the set time frame is considerable. In order to limit their financial risk, venture capital firms invest in companies in multiple rounds, rather than providing the total investment required from the start. Staging the capital contributions through different investment rounds allows investors to assess the company's progress in terms of value increase prior to each new investment round and enables them to take timely measures if the viability of the company is at stake. It also offers several opportunities to minimise losses by discontinuing the project. If the value of the company increases, multiple rounds make it possible to issue equity at a higher price in each round, thus enabling the shareholders to capitalise on the progress they have achieved between consecutive rounds.

The time between rounds depends on the time required for the company to achieve value- increasing *milestones* (see *section 3 – Milestones*, of chapter 4) and typically ranges from 1 to 2 years. Over time, the burn rate (rate at which the company uses up its available funds) of the company tends to increase, meaning that more money will be required to bridge an additional period of similar length. Consequently, since the investment risks generally decrease as the company moves into a more mature phase, larger amounts are usually committed in later rounds.

FIGURE 1: VENTURE CAPITAL INVESTMENTS

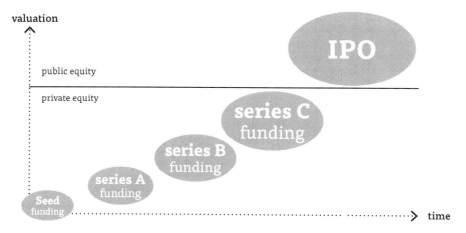

Investors investing in each round of financing will negotiate investment terms reflecting the specific investment risks they perceive. Typically, they will not accept terms that are less favourable than the terms negotiated in earlier rounds. Most of the rights negotiated in a financing are attached to the *(preferred)* shares issued in that specific round. To distinguish between these different rights, each round will typically have its own series *(class)* of shares, starting with Seed funding, followed by the Series A investment round and after that as many other rounds as are necessary until an IPO or acquisition of the company takes place.

In practice, the investment process can be a time-consuming and costly affair. Legal costs can (and usually do) form a large part of the costs involved in that process. More often than not, the legal costs will be higher than anticipated. The best way to avoid excessive legal costs is by being well prepared. Only involve a lawyer in matters where he truly has an added value. Take your time in selecting a good lawyer with solid experience in venture capital transactions (you don't want to pay a lawyer for providing him with an on-the-job venture capital learning experience).

If you are planning on doing a venture capital transaction in a country in which you have not been active before, it is important to ensure support from knowledgeable advisors. Not doing so could result in costly misunderstandings due to (for example legal) differences between the country you are used to working in and the "new" country.

The time required to raise money differs from case to case, but generally speaking the whole process, from the first cup of coffee with the venture capitalist to closing of the transaction, will take four to eight months. Venture capital investors usually want to assess a company's performance over a certain period of time, rather than base their investment decision on the company's performance at one moment only. So the advice to start-ups is: start drinking cups of coffee with venture capital investors as soon as possible. Since the time between financing rounds is usually no more than one or two years, as set out above, investor interaction should basically be a continuous activity for any start-up's CEO.

FIGURE 2: LIFE CYCLE OF START-UP

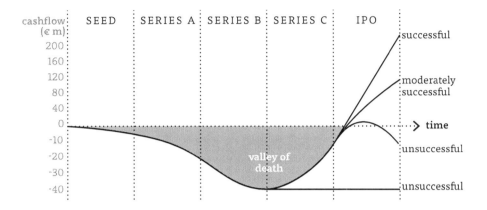

This is what venture capital is all about: the financing of loss-making companies to help them through the equity gap (also called: 'valley of death'). The equity gap arises from the perception that high risk, high transactional and monitoring costs, and the long development trajectories associated with early-stage ventures make them unattractive for investment. Due to this perception, most investors favour ventures in later stages of development that can demonstrate marketing and financial history. Venture capital investors, however, have a different perspective. They believe the risk involved in early stage investment is acceptable in view of the potentially high returns that can be realized if a start-up company becomes successful.

2 NEW WAVE ENERGY CASE STUDY

In this book, the fictional company *New Wave Energy* will be used as the basis for the explanation of the terms of a typical term sheet. *New Wave Energy* is the brainchild of Bill Pear. Bill Pear is a thirty-eight-year-old engineer who is in the process of developing a new 'green' energy technology using ocean waves as energy source. If successful, the technology is expected to have huge commercial value. In this chapter we follow the company through its various stages of funding, from incorporation to IPO, each described in a separate paragraph. The financial statements of *New Wave Energy*, which include a profit and loss account and cash flow statement at each funding round, are attached as Annex 2. Please have a look at those financial statements before reading any further. At the end of each paragraph we have included a *capitalisation table* (cap table) that shows the changes in shareholdings. The graphs included in this chapter represent the financial lifecycle of the company up to and including an IPO, showing cash flow and the company's valuation over the various points in time.

2.1 INCORPORATION

Over the last year and a half, Bill Pear has divided his time equally between his academic work at a university and the development of his revolutionary new energy technology. A year ago, Bill's thirty-five-year-old friend Peter Singh, who – like Bill – is an engineer, joined forces with him. Both Bill and Peter have now saved enough money to exclusively focus on the development of the technology for about a year. Bill has decided it is now time to incorporate a company from which Peter and he will continue the development of the technology on a fulltime basis. Since Bill has come up with the idea of the new technology and has spent most time developing it, they agree he will receive 60% of the shares. Peter will receive the remaining 40%. At incorporation, 1,000,000 common shares are issued and subscribed for at par value by Bill and Peter.

FIGURE 3: CAP TABLE NEW WAVE ENERGY AT INCORPORATION

	Common Shares	Incorporation % Holding
Bill Pear	600,000	60%
Peter Singh	400,000	40%
Total	**1,000,000**	**100%**

2.2 SEED ROUND

Now that they are working fulltime on the development of the new technology, things are speeding up. Bill and Peter are excited. They have worked very hard during the last nine months. With their new technology they will be able to offer a new, 'green', and relatively cheap source of energy. They believe they could be ready to present a prototype of their revolutionary product, the *'WaveMachine'* in about six months. However, that would require the employment of two full-time equivalents (FTEs) as well as the purchase of expensive equipment. Unfortunately, their own savings are dwindling rapidly.

FIGURE 4: SEED PHASE

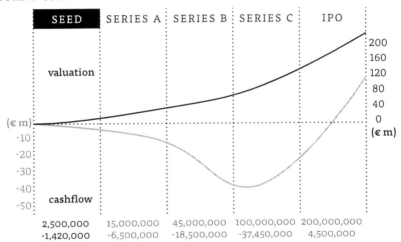

New Wave Energy needs seed funding. Seed funding is essential to bridge the first part of what is called the 'valley of death', the first stage after incorporation where risks of failure are very high. Bill manages to attract a seed venture capital fund (VC1) that is willing to invest €1,500,000 in *New Wave Energy*. It values the company at €2,500,000, a valuation that Bill and Peter agree with. After VC1 has made its investment, the 'post-money' valuation of *New Wave Energy* is €4,000,000. In exchange for its investment, the fund will receive common shares representing 38% of the shares in *New Wave Energy*. The holdings of Bill and Peter, who do not make any new investment, will dilute to 38% and 25% respectively. The capitalisation table (cap table) pre-seed and post-seed financing reads as follows:

FIGURE 5: CAP TABLE SEED ROUND

	Pre financing		SEED ROUND		Post financing	
	Common Shares	% Holding	Amount €	Shares issued	Total # Shares	% Holding
Bill Pear	600,000	60%			600,000	38%
Peter Singh	400,000	40%			400,000	25%
VC 1		0%	€1,500,000	600,000	600,000	38%
Total	1,000,000	100%	€1,500,000	600,000	1,600,000	100%
Valuation	Pre-money		€2,500,000	Price per share		€2.50
	Investment round		€1,500,000			
	Post-money		**€4,000,000**			

2.3 SERIES A ROUND – EARLY STAGE PHASE

Several months after the seed investment round, a prototype of *New Wave Energy's* revolutionary new product, the *WaveMachine*, is presented. This is an important milestone (a *value inflection point*) that will increase the company's valuation. Although many challenges must be overcome before the prototype can be transformed into a product that is ready for production, the presentation is a success. Many renowned energy experts are impressed by the potential of the revolutionary new green energy technology used in the *WaveMachine*. The interest for *New Wave Energy's* product and the technology incorporated in it is substantial. *New Wave Energy*, however, still has a long way to go before it will have a product that is ready for production. Substantial investments will have to be made in order to further develop *New Wave Energy's* promising new product. Additional engineers need to be hired, all sorts of high-tech equipment and machines must be purchased, a large development lab and offices will have to be rented, etc. In short, *New Wave Energy* needs a substantial amount of new funds (see the profit and loss account and cash flow statement of *New Wave Energy*, which is attached as Annex 2).

FIGURE 6: EARLY STAGE PHASE

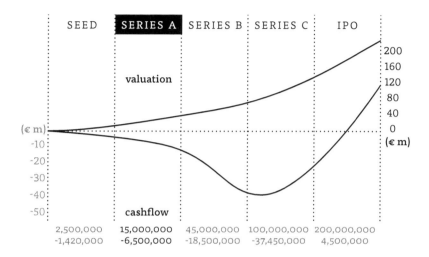

A Series A round is initiated. In this round, a new venture capital firm, VC2, becomes involved in *New Wave Energy*. VC2 is impressed by *New Wave Energy's* new technology and product, its team and the success they have had so far. It strongly believes *New Wave Energy's* new technology and product can become extremely profitable, provided they are developed professionally and the company has access to sufficient resources. It also believes substantial investments will have to be made and the organisation of *New Wave Energy* will have to be radically changed in order to ensure a professional and efficient development of the product. VC2 has a strong track record in green energy ventures and believes it is ideally equipped to assist *New Wave Energy* in this important phase of the company.

VC2 and *New Wave Energy* agree on *New Wave Energy's* business plan and determine that an investment of €8 million is required. VC2 will invest €6 million and VC1 will co-invest €2 million under the same terms and conditions. With this investment they believe *New Wave Energy* should be able to dramatically increase the company's value in the next 18 months. They also agree on a new pre-money valuation of €15 million. *New Wave Energy* will use the €8 million investment to hire additional engineers, purchase equipment and machines, rent a large development facility and offices, etc.

VC2 is only willing to invest if it receives certain financial and controlling rights over the company. These rights will be attached to a special class of preferred shares (Series A Preferred Shares) to be issued to VC2 and VC1 in the Series A round. Furthermore, as a condition to the investment, it is agreed that *New Wave Energy* will set up an *employee stock option pool* (ESOP) immediately after the investment round is closed. The ESOP should equal approximately 5% of the outstanding shares, post-money. The shares reserved under the ESOP will be used as an incentive tool for the employees. The terms and conditions of the financing and the structure of the Series A investment round are set out in a term sheet drafted by VC2 and submitted to CEO Bill Pear and the other shareholders. This term sheet is set out in full in Chapter 3 and serves as the basis for this book.

After its investment, VC2 will hold 25% of the outstanding shares on a fully diluted basis (including the ESOP). None of the initial shareholders other than VC1 invested any capital during this investment round. Consequently, the holdings of each of the initial shareholders are diluted. The post-money valuation of *New Wave Energy* after the Series A round is €23 million.

FIGURE 7: CAP TABLE SERIES A ROUND

	Pre financing		SERIES A			Post financing	
	Common Shares	% Holding	Amount €	Shares issued	Issuance ESOP	Total # Shares	% Holding
Bill Pear	600,000	38%				600,000	23%
Peter Singh	400,000	25%				400,000	16%
VC 1	600,000	38%	€2,000,000	213,333		813,333	32%
VC 2			€6,000,000	640,000		640,000	25%
ESOP					125,000	125,000	5%
Total	**1,600,000**	**100%**	**€8,000,000**	**853,333**	**125,000**	**2,578,333**	**100%**
Valuation	Pre-money		€15,000,000	Price per share		€9.38	
	Investment round		€8,000,000				
	Post-money		**€23,000,000**				

2.4 SERIES B ROUND – GROWTH PHASE

One year after the Series A round, the *WaveMachine* is in production. The company is also generating some income from technology license fees. At this point, additional funds are required to further develop the production and to expand *New Wave Energy's* sales organisation.

Although all parties involved feel *New Wave Energy* is performing extremely well, the company has so far been 'burning' cash; earnings are still modest. Substantial investments will have to be made in order to enable *New Wave Energy* to increase production of the *WaveMachine* and to expand the company's marketing & sales organisation. If these investments are made, it is believed *New Wave Energy* can reach break-even within two years (see Annex 2 for the profit and loss account and cash flow statement of *New Wave Energy* at this stage of financing).

FIGURE 8: GROWTH PHASE

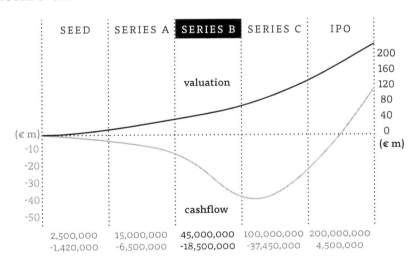

Currently, the company is running out of cash. Additional capital is required. In order to obtain this additional capital, a new investment round is initiated. Based on the business plan and some initial due diligence a syndicate formed by two venture capital firms (VC3 and VC4) submits a term sheet to finance the company with €15 million in a €20 million Series B round. After several rounds of negotiations, the pre-money valuation is set at €45 million. VC1 and VC2 decide to provide respectively €1 million and €4 million of the remaining €5 million. The investors perceive the reaching of the initial production phase as an important milestone that will drive up the valuation of New Wave Energy and prepare it for a new round of financing.

VC3 and VC4 and New Wave Energy and the other investors come to an agreement and the Series B round is closed in accordance with the term sheet. New preferred shares are issued (Series B Shares) at a fully diluted price of €17.45 per share. All parties agree that the ESOP will be increased post-money in order to partially compensate the employees for the dilution they incurred because of this round. After the increase of the ESOP, VC3 and VC4 will each hold 11% of the outstanding capital on a fully diluted basis.

FIGURE 9: CAP TABLE SERIES B

	Pre financing				SERIES B			Post financing	
	Common Shares	Pref Series A+B	Total # shares	% Holding	Amount €	Shares issued	Issuance ESOP	Total # Shares	% Holding
Bill Pear	600,000	-	600,000	23%				600,000	16%
Peter Singh	400,000	-	400,000	16%				400,000	11%
VC 1	600,000	213,333	813,333	32%	€1,000,000	57,296		870,629	23%
VC 2		640,000	640,000	25%	€4,000,000	229,185		869,185	23%
VC 3					€7,500,000	429,722		429,722	11%
VC 4					€7,500,000	429,722		429,722	11%
ESOP	125,000	-	125,000	5%			75,000	200,000	5%
Total	1,725,000	853,333	2,578,333	100%	€20,000,000	1,145,925	75,000	3,799,258	100%

Valuation	Pre-money	€45,000,000	Price per share	€17.45
	Investment round	€20,000,000		
	Post-money	**€65,000,000**		

2.5 SERIES C ROUND – FURTHER GROWTH

Two years after the Series B round, all is going well for the company. Production and sales of the *WaveMachine* have increased substantially and two other green energy products are being developed. Furthermore, *New Wave Energy* has recently entered into a strategic partnership with a large multinational original equipment manufacturer (OEM). Under this strategic partnership the OEM uses *New Wave Energy's* revolutionary technology to produce (under its own brand name) a green energy product similar to the *WaveMachine*. Thanks to the revenues from the *WaveMachine* and the strategic partnership, *New Wave Energy* has nearly reached revenue break-even. The company's cash-flow deficit is at its peak but will, from now on, decrease steadily. This is another important value inflection point.

FIGURE 10: FURTHER GROWTH PHASE

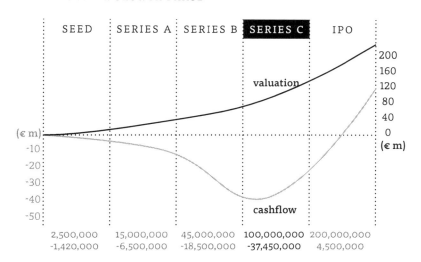

At this point, additional funds are required to further expand *New Wave Energy's* sales organisation, set up offices in two other continents and perhaps the acquisition of a competitor. With this additional financing, the company should be able to build sufficient substance to successfully file for an initial public offering (IPO) on an international stock exchange. Together with the investors VC1 and VC2, *New Wave Energy* determines that it requires at least €40 million to reach its goals. A new business plan is drafted and submitted to several potential investors. VC5 submits a term sheet to finance the company with €25 million in a €40 million Series

C round. The pre-money valuation is set at €100 million. VC3 and VC4 decide to provide the remaining €15 million. The ESOP will be increased to 16% post-money to attract new highly skilled people and to motivate the management to prepare the company for an IPO at the earliest practical possibility. After the investment of €40 million, the valuation will be €140 million.

FIGURE 11: CAP TABLE SERIES C ROUND

	Pre financing				SERIES C			Post financing	
	Common Shares	Pref Series A+B	Total # shares	% Holding	Amount €	Shares issued	Issuance ESOP	Total # Shares	% Holding
Bill Pear	600,000	-	600,000	16%				600,000	10%
Peter Singh	400,000	-	400,000	11%				400,000	7%
VC 1	600,000	270,629	870,629	23%	-	-		870,629	14%
VC 2		869,185	869,185	23%	-	-		869,185	14%
VC 3		429,722	429,722	11%	€5,000,000	189,963		619,685	10%
VC 4		429,722	429,722	11%	€10,000,000	379,926		809,648	13%
VC 5		-			€25,000,000	949,815		949,815	16%
ESOP	200,000	-	200,000	5%			700,000	900,000	15%
Total	1,800,000	1,999,258	3,799,258	100%	€40,000,000	1,519,704	700,000	6,018,962	100%

Valuation	Pre-money	€100,000,000	Price per share	€26.32
	Investment round	€40,000,000		
	Post-money	**€140,000,000**		

2.6 IPO (INITIAL PUBLIC OFFERING)

New Wave Energy has reached revenue break-even and is about to reach cash flow break-even as well. It has developed its own production facility for the *WaveMachine*, generated a pipeline of new products and established a solid sales organisation. It requires new money for the expansion of its marketing activities two other continents, the acquisition of competitors and expansion of the asset-heavy production facility. The company has approached an investment bank for advice on its potential to go public. The investment bank agrees that the company can successfully file for a listing and is hired to assist *New Wave Energy* in this complicated process. *New Wave Energy's* senior management, along with representatives from the investment bank, visit potential (institutional) investors to determine the optimal valuation of the company for the purpose of raising the approximately €75 million required to achieve the company's future goals. Based on the feedback during this so-called 'road show', *New Wave Energy* will be introduced at a valuation of €200 million. However, before the IPO can take place, all regulatory requirements must be fulfilled and all preferred shares must be converted into common shares on a 1:1 basis since no dilutive round or event leading to an adjustment of the conversion ratio has occurred (see *section 13 – Automatic Conversion*, of chapter 4). The price per share has increased since the Seed round from €2.50 to €33.23 immediately prior to the IPO. In order to create shares with better tradability, the shares are split.

At the IPO, new shares will be issued and sold to the public. The existing shareholders will not be allowed to sell or transfer their shares during a lock-up period. Such a period is typically six to twelve months for the investors and may be longer for the management board (the underwriting bank(s) and/or the stock exchange or (other) regulatory authorities usually require(s) a lock-up period).

In general, the involvement of the venture capital investor ends at this point. The controlling rights and financial preferences attached to his preferred shares have terminated upon conversion and his nominee at the company's supervisory board will step down from the board, or will do so in the following months, in order to enable the investor to sell his shares on the stock exchange without restriction of any insider trading rules.

FIGURE 12: CAP TABLE AT IPO

	Pre financing					Post IPO	
	Total Shares	Conversion & Stock split	% Holding	Amount €	Shares issued	Total # Shares	% Holding
Bill Pear	600,000	1,329,133	10%			1,329,133	7%
Peter Singh	400,000	886,089	7%			886,089	5%
VC 1	870,629	1,928,636	14%			1,928,636	11%
VC 2	869,185	1,925,437	14%			1,925,437	11%
VC 3	619,685	1,372,739	10%			1,372,739	7%
VC 4	809,648	1,793,550	13%			1,793,550	10%
VC 5	949,815	2,104,050	16%			2,104,050	11%
Flotation	-	-		75,000,000	5,000,000	5,000,000	27%
ESOP	900,000	1,993,699	15%			1,993,699	11%
Total	6,018,962	13,333,333	100%	75,000,000	5,000,000	18,333,333	100%

Valuation	IPO Pricing	€200,000,000	Price per share (before split)	€33.23
	Investment round	€75,000,000	Price per share (after split)	€15.00
	Post-money	**€275,000,000**	Split Ratio	2.21522103

FIGURE 13: IPO

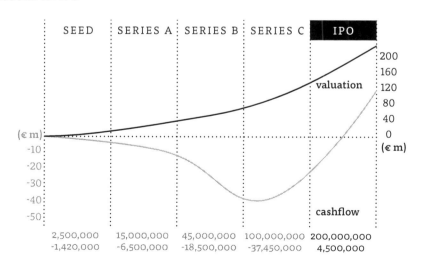

3 NEW WAVE ENERGY TERM SHEET

Set out below is the term sheet submitted by VC2 to *New Wave Energy* as mentioned in *section 3*, of chapter 2. This term sheet will constitute the basis for this book. Each clause of the term sheet will be explained in more detail in the following chapters.

NEW WAVE ENERGY

SUMMARY OF PROPOSED TERMS AND CONDITIONS
SERIES A CONVERTIBLE PREFERRED SHARES

This term sheet (the "**Term Sheet**") summarises the principal terms and conditions with respect to the proposed investment by VC2 and VC1 in exchange for Series A convertible preferred shares to be issued by *New Wave Energy*.

OFFERING TERMS

Issuer	New Wave Energy (the "Company")
Amount of Financing	€8,000,000
Milestones	The amount of financing is payable in two equal tranches. The first tranche is payable at the Closing, the second tranche will be payable upon the closing of a license deal for the WaveMachine which generates a license fee of at least €10,000 per month.
Investors	VC2 (lead investor) will invest €6,000,000. The existing investor, VC1, will invest the remaining €2,000,000. VC1 and VC2 are jointly referred to as the "Investors".
Type of Security	Series A convertible preferred shares (the "Series A Shares"). The Series A Shares are senior to the outstanding common shares (the "Common Shares").

Share Price and Valuation	€9.38 per share representing a fully diluted pre-money valuation of €15,000,000.
Capital Structure	The attached capitalisation table (Appendix [__]) details all of the securities that will be outstanding immediately prior to and after the Closing.
Anticipated Closing Date	60 days after the execution of this Term Sheet (the "Closing").
Dividends	The Series A Shares will carry a dividend in preference to the Common Shares of 5% of the original purchase price per annum, which will accrue and cumulate annually and will be payable only if declared.
Redemption	At the election of the holders of at least 75% of the Series A Shares, subject to any restrictions under applicable law, the Company will redeem all outstanding Series A Shares in full, at any time after the fifth anniversary of the Closing. Such redemption will be at a price equal to the original purchase price (as adjusted for stock splits, stock dividends and the like) plus any accrued and unpaid dividends.
Voluntary Conversion	A holder of Series A Shares will have the right to convert Series A Shares, or any part of such shares including declared dividends, at the option of the holder, at any time, into Common Shares. The total number of Common Shares into which each Series A Share may be converted will be determined by dividing the original purchase price by the conversion price. The conversion price will initially be equal to the original purchase price. The conversion price will however be subject to a proportional adjustment for share dividends, splits, combinations and similar events and in accordance with the 'Anti-Dilution' clause.

Automatic Conversion The Series A Shares will automatically be converted into Common Shares at the then applicable conversion price upon: (i) the closing of a firmly underwritten public offering with a price per share of at least 8 times the original purchase price and proceeds to the Company of not less than €100 million (a "Qualified Offering"), or (ii) the written consent of the holders of 75% of the Series A Shares.

Anti-Dilution In the event that the Company issues new shares or securities convertible into or exchangeable for shares at a purchase price lower than the applicable conversion price of the Series A Shares, then the conversion price of the Series A Shares will be subject to a full ratchet adjustment, reducing the applicable conversion price of the Series A Shares to the price at which the new shares are (to be) issued.

The anti-dilution adjustment will not apply in the event of issuance of Common Shares issued or issuable to employees, consultants or directors of the Company directly or pursuant to the ESOP (as set out in the 'Employee Pool' clause) that have been approved by the Supervisory Board.

Pay-to-Play Holders of Preferred Shares are required to participate in any dilutive issuance including the Series A Financing to the extent of their pro rata equity interest in the Preferred Shares, unless the participation requirement is waived for all Preferred Shareholders by the Supervisory Board.

In the event that a holder of Preferred Shares fails to participate in accordance with the previous paragraph, the Preferred Shares held by such shareholder will automatically lose their anti-dilution and liquidation rights.

Liquidation Preference

In the event of a liquidation or winding up of the Company, the holders of Series A Shares will be entitled to receive, in preference to the holders of the Common Shares, payment of an amount equal to the original purchase price per Series A Share, plus any accumulated and unpaid dividends.

If there are insufficient assets or proceeds to pay such amount to the holders of Series A Shares in full, the amount available will be paid on a pro rata basis between the holders of Series A Shares.

Thereafter any remaining assets or proceeds will be distributed pro rata among the holders of Common Shares and the holders of Series A Shares (the latter on an 'as-if' converted basis).

A reorganisation, consolidation, merger of the Company, sale or issue of shares or any other event pursuant to which the shareholders of the Company will have less than 51% of the voting power of the surviving or acquiring corporation, or the sale, lease, transfer or other disposition of all or substantially all of the Company's assets will be deemed to be a liquidation or winding up for the purposes of the liquidation preference (a "Deemed Liquidation Event"), thereby triggering the liquidation preferences described above.

Favourable Terms

The terms herein, other than valuation, are subject to a review of the rights, preferences and restrictions pertaining to the existing shares in the Company. Any changes necessary to conform such existing shares to this Term Sheet will be made at the Closing as necessary in order to ensure that holders of existing Common Shares will not have rights more favourable than those of the holders of Series A Shares.

Board Representation The supervision of the policies by the Management Board and all other tasks and duties as assigned to it will be entrusted to the supervisory board ("Supervisory Board"), which at Closing will consist of three members comprised of (i) one member elected upon the nomination of the holders of the Series A Shares; (ii) one member upon the nomination of Bill Pear and Peter Singh (the "Founders"); and (iii) one member who has specific expertise in the Company's field of business nominated by a majority of all shareholders and who is mutually acceptable to the Founders and Investors.

The Company will take out D&O insurance in the amount of at least €5 million per occurrence.

Voting Rights The holders of Series A Shares will vote together with the holders of Common Shares and not as a separate class, except as specifically provided herein or as otherwise required by law. Each Series A Share will have a number of votes equal to the number of Common Shares issuable upon conversion of such Series A Share.

Consent Rights The Company's articles of association or any other constitutive corporate documents will be amended to contain restrictions making certain resolutions of the Management Board with a material effect on the Company's operations or management subject to the prior approval of the Supervisory Board. In addition, these documents will contain restrictions making certain resolutions of the general meeting of shareholders (e.g. resolutions regarding the structure and capitalisation of the Company) subject to the prior approval of the holders of Series A Shares.

Registration Rights	The holders of Series A Shares will have normal registration rights including demand registration rights, unlimited 'piggyback' registration rights, S-3 registration rights, transfer of registration rights, proportionate underwriter cut-backs, and other typical registration rights, all at the expense of the Company. In the event that the public offering as referred to in this 'Registration Rights' clause will or has taken place on a stock exchange outside the U.S, then the holders of Registrable Securities will be entitled to registration rights equivalent to the rights and obligations contained in this 'Registration Rights' clause (or as equivalent as possible given differences in applicable law).
Representations and Warranties	The investment agreement or a separate representation and warranties agreement will include standard representations and warranties granted by the Company and existing shareholders, including, but not expressly limited to: (i) organisation and good standing; (ii) capitalisation structure; (iii) due authorisation; (iv) valid share issuance; (v) governmental consents; (vi) no company litigation; (vii) ownership or exclusive license of intellectual property rights; (viii) employees; (ix) pension plans; (x) assurances of full disclosure and accuracy of information provided; (xi) good title to all assets; (xii) tax; (xiii) accuracy of financial statements; (xiv) absence of adverse developments; and (xv) material contracts.

Information Rights	Any holder of Series A Shares will be granted access to Company facilities and personnel during normal business hours and with reasonable advance notification. The Company will deliver to such Investor (i) un-audited financial statements within 120 days after the end of the calendar year; (ii) and monthly financial statements within 20 days after such period, and other information as determined by the Supervisory Board; (iii) thirty days prior to the end of each fiscal year, a comprehensive operating budget forecasting the Company's revenues, expenses, and cash position on a month-to-month basis for the upcoming fiscal year; and (iv) promptly following the end of each quarter, an up-to-date capitalisation table, certified by the CFO. The foregoing provisions will terminate upon a Qualified Offering.
Use of Proceeds	The Company will apply the net proceeds of the sale of the Series A Shares exclusively to the development and operation of the Company in accordance with a business plan and budget to be approved by the Investors prior to the Closing.
Pre-emptive Rights	Without prejudice to the 'Anti-Dilution' clause, if the Company proposes to offer equity securities, or securities convertible into or exchangeable for shares, the holders of Series A Shares will be entitled to purchase such securities in an amount sufficient to allow the holders them to retain their fully diluted ownership of the Company.

The pre-emptive right will not apply in the event of issuances of (i) Common Shares issued or issuable to employees, consultants or directors of the Company directly or pursuant to the ESOP (as set out in the 'Employee Pool' clause) that have been approved by the Supervisory Board; (ii) Common Shares issued or issuable upon conversion of the Preferred Shares; (iii) Common Shares issued or issuable in connection with a merger, acquisition, combination, consolidation or other reorganisation involving the Company approved by the Supervisory Board of the Company; (iv) Common Shares issued or issuable in connection with (a) any borrowings from a commercial lending institution, (b) the lease of equipment or property by the Company, or (c) strategic partnerships and/or licensing relationships, so long as such transactions are approved by the Supervisory Board; and (v) Common Shares issued or issuable (a) in a Qualified Offering before or in connection with which all outstanding Preferred Shares will be converted to Common Shares or (b) upon exercise of warrants or rights granted to underwriters in connection with such a Qualified Offering.

Rights of First Refusal Holders of Series A Shares have a right of first refusal with respect to any shares proposed to be sold by a shareholder, at the same price and on the same terms as offered, with a right of over-subscription for holders of Series A Shares of shares un-subscribed by the other holders of Series A Shares. Such right of first refusal will terminate upon the earlier of (i) a Qualified Offering; or (ii) a sale or merger of the Company.

Co-Sale Right Before any shareholder may sell shares in the Company, after having observed the terms and procedures of the 'Right of first Refusal' clause, he will give the other Shareholders an opportunity to participate in such sale on a pro rata basis.

Drag-Along Right The holders of a 75% majority of Series A Shares may require a sale of the entire issued share capital of the Company.

Management Board The management of the Company will be entrusted to the management board (the "Management Board") consisting at Closing of Bill Pear as chief executive officer and Peter Singh as chief financial officer. Any new management board member or senior company officers will not receive an offer of employment without the approval of the Supervisory Board. The Company will, on a 'best effort' basis, hire a chief business development officer within the six-month period following the Closing.

Employee Pool Upon the Closing, the Company will reserve up to 5% of the post-money outstanding shares for issuance to employees, directors and consultants (the "Reserved Employee Shares"). The Reserved Employee Shares will be issued from time to time under an employee share option plan (the "ESOP") as approved by the Supervisory Board.

Vesting Scheme All Reserved Employee Shares will be subject to vesting as follows: 25% to vest at the end of the first year following their issuance, with the remaining 75% to vest monthly over the next three years.

Founder's Shares Upon Closing, 1,000,000 of the Company's issued and outstanding Common Shares will be held by the Founders (the "Founders' Shares"). The Founders' Shares will be made subject to a similar vesting scheme as set forth in the 'Vesting Scheme' clause, provided that the vesting period will begin as of the Closing.

Employment Relationships	The Company has or will have prior to the Closing: employment agreements, proprietary information and inventions agreements, one year non-competition and non-solicitation agreements, and non-disclosure agreements with the Founders and key employees in a form reasonably acceptable to the Investors.
Lock-Up	At no time prior to the fifth anniversary of the Closing will any Founder dispose of any shares in the Company in any manner, except with the written consent of two-thirds of the holders of Series A Shares. This lock-up will in any case lapse at the consummation of a Qualified IPO, trade sale or other liquidity event.
Non-Competition/Non-Solicitation	Prior to Closing, each Founder and key employee will enter into a one-year non-competition and non-solicitation agreement in a form reasonably acceptable to the Investors.
Non-Disclosure Agreement	Prior to Closing, each Founder, and each officer, employee and consultant with access to the Company's confidential information/trade secrets will enter into a non-disclosure agreement in a form reasonably acceptable to the Investors.
Assignment Inventions	Prior to Closing, each Founder and key employee will enter into a proprietary rights assignment agreement in a form reasonably acceptable to the Investors. Such agreement will contain, inter alia, appropriate terms and conditions under which each Founder and key employee will assign to the Company their relevant existing patents and patent applications and other intellectual property rights as defined by the Company's business plan.

Key Man Insurance Within three months of the Closing, the Company will procure a life insurance policy for the Founders in the amount of €1 million per person (or such lesser amount as approved by the Investors). The Company will be named as the beneficiary of the policies.

Agreements at Closing The purchase of the Series A Shares will be made pursuant to an Investment and Shareholders' Agreement acceptable to the Investors and containing, inter alia, appropriate representations, warranties as referenced in the 'Representation and Warranties' clause and covenants of the Company, Management Board and existing shareholders, where appropriate reflecting the provisions set forth herein and appropriate conditions of the Closing.

Fees and Expenses The Company will pay reasonable fees and expenses incurred by the Investors in connection with (the preparation of) the transaction contemplated by this Term Sheet, including (but not limited to) expenses in connection with the preparation of legal documentation and the conduct of due diligence investigation(s) payable at the Closing or payable as soon as the Company elects not to proceed with the transaction contemplated by this Term Sheet.

Confidentiality The parties will keep strictly confidential the fact that they have entered into negotiations concerning the transactions contemplated by this Term Sheet and the contents of such negotiations and of this Term Sheet.

Exclusivity/ No-Shop

The Company agrees to work in good faith expeditiously towards the Closing. The Company and the Founders agree (a) to discontinue any discussions with other parties concerning any investment in the Company, (b) not to take any action to solicit, initiate, encourage or assist the submission of any proposal, negotiation or offer from any person or entity other than the Investors relating to the sale or issuance, of any of the capital shares of the Company, and (c) to notify the Investors promptly of any inquiries by any third parties in regards to the foregoing.

This provision 'Exclusivity/No-Shop' will be in force until six weeks after the execution of this Term Sheet. Thereafter this exclusivity period will automatically continue for a period of two weeks (revolving) unless either the Company or the Investors decide to end the discussions by way of a written notice to the other party at least five days prior to the ending of such exclusivity period.

Governing Law

This Term Sheet and all other agreements resulting from this Term Sheet will be exclusively governed by the law of the country in which the Company's seat is located.

Insofar as permissible by law, exclusive jurisdiction for all disputes arising from and in connection with the present Term Sheet will be the seat of the Company.

Non-binding Character

Except as otherwise specifically provided herein, the parties to this Term Sheet expressly agree that no binding obligations will be created until a definitive agreement is executed with the requisite formality and delivered by both parties.

Notwithstanding the foregoing, the clauses entitled 'Fees and Expenses', 'Confidentiality', 'Exclusivity/ No-Shop', and 'Governing Law' will be binding upon execution of this Term Sheet.

Indemnities The Company and the Investors will each indemnify the other for any finder's fees for which either is responsible.

Conditions Precedent The Closing is subject to the following conditions precedent:

(1) satisfactory completion of financial, tax and legal due diligence; (2) no material adverse change in the financial condition or the prospects of the Company as mentioned in the business plan [and any documents sent to the Investors]; (3) negotiation and execution of legal documentation satisfactory to the Investors; (4) consent of the necessary legal majority of the Company's shareholders, and (5) final formal approval of the Investors' investment and partner committees.

Expiration This Term Sheet expires on [__] if not accepted by the Company by that date.

Signatures:

New Wave Energy
Name: ....
Title: ....

Bill Pear
Name: ....
Title: ....

Peter Singh
Name: ....
Title: ....

VC1
Name: ....
Title: ....

VC2
Name: ....
Title: ....

APPENDIX 1: CAPITALISATION TABLE NEW WAVE ENERGY

	Pre financing		SERIES A			Post financing	
	Common Shares	% Holding	Amount €	Shares issued	Issuance ESOP	Total # Shares	% Holding
Bill Pear	600,000	38%				600,000	23%
Peter Singh	400,000	25%				400,000	16%
VC 1	600,000	38%	€2,000,000	213,333		813,333	32%
VC 2			€6,000,000	640,000		640,000	25%
ESOP					125,000	125,000	5%
Total	**1,600,000**	**100%**	**€8,000,000**	**853,333**	**125,000**	**2,578,333**	**100%**
Valuation	Pre-money		€15,000,000	Price per share		€9.38	
	Investment round		€8,000,000				
	Post-money		**€23,000,000**				

4 TERMS EXPLAINED

4.1 ISSUER

In most venture capital transactions, the type of legal entity in which the investors will invest, is not an issue. Normally it would be a company with limited liability and a capital divided in shares. This type of company exists in every jurisdiction, albeit under different names and subject to different specific laws and regulations.

Examples of limited liability companies include S.A. (*Société Anonyme*) in France, A.G. (*Aktiengesellschaft*) and GmbH (*Gesellschaft mit beschränkter Haftung*) in Germany and Switzerland, S.p.A. (*Società per Azioni*) in Italy, B.V. (*Besloten Vennootschap*) and N.V. (*Naamloze Vennootschap*) in the Netherlands, S.A. (*Sociedad Anónima*) and S.R.L. (*Sociedad de Responsabildad Limitada*) in Spain, Ltd. (*Limited Liability Company*) in the UK and Inc. (*Corporation*) and LLC (*Limited Liability Company*) in the US.

In the past ten years, many European jurisdictions have made their limited liability company law more flexible. Where in the past it could take a couple of weeks to incorporate a limited liability company, nowadays in most European countries it will take only one or two days. Furthermore, many jurisdictions have abolished their minimum capital rules or made them far less burdensome than they used to be.

By investing in a company's equity capital, the investor becomes an owner of the company. Consequently, an increase or decrease in the value of the company will be reflected in a pro rata increase or decrease in the value of his investment (shares). From an investors' risk perspective, one of the most important benefits of investing in a company with limited liability is that he is not liable for the company's debts and obligations beyond the amount he paid for his shares. Furthermore, the concept of the legal personality of legal entities provides personal protection to individual managers from claims against the company (a legal liability of the legal entity is not necessarily a legal liability of any of its managers).

Obviously, the legislation applying to limited liability companies varies from one jurisdiction to another. It is therefore important to determine which matters are covered by the applicable law and which matters need to be dealt with separately (e.g. in a term sheet or shareholders' agreement).

For the purpose of this book, we will assume that the company in which the investors will invest is a company with limited liability.

Issuer: [name company], (the "**Company**").

4.2 AMOUNT OF FINANCING

In the introduction, we touched on the typical funding stages that a start-up company passes through in the course of its life. Each of these stages normally starts and ends with a new financing round that is intended to enable the company to reach its next stage. During each stage, the company and its management should work to achieve significant business developments in order be able to successfully raise and close a next round of financing.

The amount of financing is mainly driven by market circumstances. Ideally, the amount of financing in each round is barely sufficient for the company to realise adequate progress. If the amount of financing is too small, the company will run out of funds before the fruits of the previous round can be presented convincingly. Thus raising funds in the next round at a higher valuation will be likely to fail, especially since the aim is to raise funds at a higher value per share issued. Furthermore, with insufficient cash availability, the company has to go out fundraising more often. This is a time-consuming business that distracts from the core activity of creating real value. If on the other hand the amount of financing is more than strictly needed to achieve value-increasing milestones, the company and its management may lose focus and control of their expenditure. From the founders' perspective more financing is not always better. If possible they would rather have the company raise a limited amount of financing now, and more later on at a higher valuation. This will avoid unnecessary dilution of the founders' stake in the company. But of course no one knows what the future will bring. Financing may be available a second time, or it may not. Not 'taking the cookies when they are passed' could be a bit of a gamble.

The cash requirement of a company depends largely on its stage of development. Companies that are more mature, require larger amounts of financing. In other words, larger amounts of financing are generally committed in later rounds.

Amount of Financing:	€[___] million (the "**Series [●] Financing**").

4.3 MILESTONES

In certain types of transactions, the investor may wish to work with milestones. It improves his internal rate of return (the later you invest, the better your IRR will be) and diminishes the risk of losing all his money if the company goes bankrupt before the milestone date. Milestones are pre-agreed targets that are crucial to the valuation of the company from the perspective of the investor, such as the completion of a prototype, the achievement of a proof of principle, a certain level of earnings, sales, or users, or the outcome of clinical trials. Often, a milestone will be a value inflection point. In other words: if a milestone is achieved, this will result in a significantly higher valuation of the company.

Milestones need not only be useful to investors. They can also help entrepreneurs. Entrepreneurs tend to focus on vision and may pay less attention to practicalities required to realise their vision. Milestones can be very useful in helping entrepreneurs focus on matters that have to be dealt with in the short term in order to enable them to realise their vision in the long term.

There are two types of milestones: (a) *investment milestones* and (b) *valuation milestones*. *Investment milestones* allow the investor to postpone payment of part of the amount committed until the pre-agreed milestones have been achieved. *Valuation milestones* do not affect the investment of the total committed amount, but result in a reallocation of ownership of the company. The extent of the adjustment of the valuation is typically linked to the amount of the perceived increase or decrease in valuation of the company if such a milestone is met or not met, respectively. The two types of milestones will be discussed in detail below.

A   **INVESTMENT MILESTONES**
If the amount of financing, or part thereof, is subject to the achievement of milestones, the investors will make an initial payment (a *first tranche*) at the closing of the deal, whereas the remaining investment amount will be paid in one or more tranches upon the company achieving pre-defined milestones. By structuring their investment in this manner, the investors are able to reduce their financial risk (if the milestone is not achieved, the investors' funding commitment ends) and increase the internal rate of return (IRR) (since they do not invest the total amount of financing at once, but spread the investment out over time).

For obvious reasons, the company will be in serious trouble if it does not achieve a milestone. The investors may refrain from further investment if they consider the achievement of a milestone essential to the future of the company. However, in most cases, in order to protect their initial investment, the investors are willing to renegotiate the deal and to commit further funding on more investor-friendly terms.

B   **VALUATION MILESTONES**
In contrast to the milestones discussed in the previous paragraph, milestones used as a trigger for adjustment of the valuation do not affect the total committed amount to be invested in the company, but will result in a reallocation of ownership of the company. The extent of the adjustment of the valuation is typically linked to the amount of the perceived increase or decrease in valuation of the company if such milestone is either met or not met.

Valuation milestones can either be negative – decreasing the valuation at which the aggregate investment will be made if a milestone is not achieved, or positive – increasing the pre-money valuation if a milestone is achieved.

By using negative valuation milestones, investors are able to offer a relatively high initial valuation and thus to make an attractive offer when more investors are competing for the deal, or to give the founders the benefit of the doubt by letting them prove their ambitious plans and valuation. If the milestones are not achieved, the valuation will retroactively be adjusted downwards and the investors will be entitled to additional shares. However, if the milestones are achieved, the high valuation will be maintained and the number of shares held by the investors will not change.

Alternatively, positive milestones, when achieved, will cause a retroactive upward adjustment of the valuation at which the investors have invested, entitling them to fewer shares than they had received at closing.

Typically, valuation milestones are used when the total amount of financing is made in one or more instalments or *tranches*. The due date of a valuation milestone can then coincide with the due date of an investment tranche. The number of shares to be issued upon payment of each tranche will depend on the achievement of a milestone. The total number of shares to be issued in exchange for all tranches will determine the overall pre-money valuation at which the investment is made.

If the total amount of financing is not payable in tranches but is to be paid in full at the closing, a retroactive adjustment of the valuation can be established by adjusting the conversion ratio of the preferred shares to common shares. The adjustment can be structured to increase the number of common shares to be issued to the investors upon conversion if the valuation goes down and vice versa, if the valuation goes up. Other mechanisms are the issue of new preferred shares to the investors if the valuation goes down, or the redemption of some of their preferred shares if the valuation is adjusted upwards. In smaller companies, shares can be reallocated by transfer of shares between the investors and common shareholders.

An alternative structure that can be used in tranched investments is the agreed postponement of part of the payment of the subscription price for the preferred shares. At the closing, the preferred shares will be issued to the investors in exchange for only part of the subscription price. The remainder of the subscription price will be payable in full only if the agreed milestones are met. If they are not met, the pre-money valuation will be automatically adjusted downward. In certain jurisdictions or in respect to certain types of entities the full subscription price (being the nominal value plus all share premiums) must be paid at issuance and cannot be postponed.

C   FINAL REMARKS

Considering the possible consequences of the use of milestones and the disparate interests of the investors and the founders, it is generally very important that the milestones are well defined.

Furthermore, it should be clear who decides whether a milestone has been achieved. This could be a corporate body (e.g. the meeting of preferred shareholders (i.e. the investors), the general meeting of shareholders or the supervisory board), or the decision could be left up to the parties (e.g. the company and the investors). In the latter case, if the parties can't agree whether a milestone has been achieved, this will have to be decided on in ultimate resort by the competent court. Since the investors are considered to be biased and the supervisory board is required to act in the interest of the company (and not necessarily in the interest of the investors), the election of a third party expert(s) may be a solution if there is disagreement on this issue.

Negotiation tips:
- Keep the definition of milestones simple and concrete. Avoid vagueness; for example "the successful commencement of production" can be interpreted to mean many different things. It won't work in practice.
- Don't agree on milestones if their achievement does not seem realistic; they should be realistically achievable within the set timeframe.
- You could consider including a mechanism that will make a reasonable adjustment of the milestones possible, if, at some point in the future (and with the approval of the investors) the company's strategy is changed.

Milestones:	[Alternative 1: (investment milestone): The Series [●] Financing is payable in [___] tranches of €[___] subject to the achievement of the milestones set forth in Appendix [___].]
	[Alternative 2: (valuation milestone): The pre-money valuation of €[___] as referenced in the 'Share Price and Valuation' clause will be adjusted to €[___] subject to the achievement of the milestones set forth in Appendix [___].]

4.4 INVESTORS

The clause *Investors* sets out the names of the parties providing the total amount of financing. If a number of investors join together to provide the capital under the same terms (a *syndicate*), then this section of the term sheet will also indicate which investor will act as the lead investor in this financing round and which investors will co-invest with the lead investor (the *co-investors*). If the syndicate is not filled out at the time of the execution of the term sheet, the term sheet will typically allow the lead investor to invite other investors to co-invest.

The main roles of the lead investor are to build a syndicate, to structure the deal and to manage the due diligence process and the contract drafting. In most cases, the lead investor is the first investor involved in the round and often makes the largest investment in the financing round. The lead investor's active involvement in the financing, due diligence and contract drafting process typically requires him to have easy access to the company.

Venture capitalists syndicate for several reasons. The first reason is to spread the risks involved in a venture financing. By investing in a syndicate, the risk exposure of each investor is limited and more capital is available for the company's present and future cash needs. Sharing the investment also allows the investors to build a larger and more diverse investment portfolio. Syndication also gives investors the opportunity to share know-how. Sharing expertise, market intelligence and due diligence enables the investors to make a better assessment of the company's business plan and technology, which should lead to a superior investment decision. It further allows the investors to validate their investment decision. Each investor's investment decision will be confirmed if more investors are willing to invest in the company. Another benefit of investing in syndication is to get to know other venture capitalists and to build up a network within the venture capital community, which should lead to an increased and better deal flow.

Seed financing, generally between €100,000 and €2,000,000, used to be the domain of business angels rather than venture capital funds. Over the past ten years more and more venture capital funds have entered the market. This has led to more venture capital funds focussing on the very early stage. These funds are usually referred to as Seed Funds. However, angels still play an important role in seed financing, in particular in countries with many successful serial entrepreneurs who want to re-invest part of the fortunes they have made. Sometimes these angels bundle their capital and form a seed venture capital fund that invests in multiple start-up companies. Seed Funds and angels usually require less protective terms than general (Series A+) venture capital.

Over the past few years crowdfunding has become increasingly popular as an alternative form of seed financing. There are four main forms of crowdfunding: donation, rewards, lending and equity. During the early days of crowdfunding, the rewards model was most often used. Under that model investors were paid back with products or services developed by the company. Start-ups would also sometimes utilize a pre-order model in which products were sold before they were actually produced. Donation models were also popular, especially for creative projects and charities. As interest in crowdfunding began to grow, many began to experiment with other models for securing necessary funds. Today, investors are often able to obtain an equity or debt stake in the start-up in exchange for their investments. When raising money with crowdfunding, keep in mind that you will end up with many equity- or noteholders, who may not have voting rights but will require attention in some form. Crowd-funding can be a great way to promote your product, in particular if it is a consumer product.

For the entrepreneur it is important to choose an investor whose interests run (as much as possible) in parallel with those of the company and who can help the company achieve its goals, not only financially, but also by sharing network and knowledge.

Before starting a long-term relationship with an investor, an entrepreneur should have given careful thought to many important matters. A few of those are listed below:
- What is the remaining life of the investor's fund? Venture capital funds typically have a limited lifespan (e.g. ten years). Older funds may not have sufficient time to sit out the whole ride and may want to rush an exit, or may run out of money for follow-on investments.
- What is the investor's preferred deal size? Large investment funds may want to invest a minimum amount per portfolio company. This can jeopardize a successful short-term exit of the company. Smaller investors, on the other hand, may not be able to provide sufficient funding in the future.

- Who are the investor's funders (limited partners) and what is the investor's investment mandate? Funds backed by public money often have a local or national focus. This may create a problem if the company wishes to expand abroad or can be sold to a foreign company. Be aware that venture capital funds may also be backed by strategic investors, who may have a strategic interest in your company.
- If you can choose, have one or two investors provide all required funding, rather than a handful of investors each providing a small portion. Every investor requires attention. Consequently, the more investors you have, the more time you will have to spend on investor relations. If you are dealing with a syndicate, pro-actively co-ordinate the investment process (try to be the one in the "driver's seat") in order not to lose momentum. Make sure that in the due diligence process, duplication of effort is avoided.

Investors: [name investor] as lead investor will invest €[__]. Other investors participating in the Series [●] Financing (together with the lead investor, the "**Investors**"), the amounts of their investment to be approved by the lead investor.

4.5 TYPE OF SECURITY

The *Type of Security* clause in the *New Wave Energy* term sheet (see chapter 3) indicates that the investment will be made in exchange for equity, series A convertible preferred shares to be precise. Equity is not the sole source of financing that can be provided by investors in venture capital transactions. In certain transactions, investors may provide (convertible) debt financing to companies. At times, this may be in addition to equity financing. There are essentially two types of securities: *equity securities* and *debt securities*, each with its own specific characteristics.

A EQUITY SECURITIES

Equity represents ownership in a company. Such ownership can be evidenced by and divided into equity securities, or, in more common terms – shares. In venture capital, generally there are two distinct types of shares: (i) *common* (or ordinary) shares and (ii) *preferred* shares.

I. COMMON SHARES

Basically, *common shares* are shares that carry full voting rights and are entitled to dividend payments and distributions in the case of bankruptcy of the company after all other costs and claims to the capital have been met. Common shares carry no special rights (e.g. special voting, liquidation, dividend rights) and are typically held by the founders and key employees of venture-backed companies.

II. PREFERRED SHARES

A *preferred share* is a type of share that carries certain rights that go above and beyond those conferred by common shares. In financial terms preferred shares provide their holders the right to receive payment of dividends ahead of the holders of common shares, and to take precedence over them when it comes to the distribution of the liquidation proceeds of a company. These financial preferred rights (explained in further detail in *section 10 – Dividends* and in *section 16 – Liquidation preference*, of this chapter) form the essential rights of the preferred share class.

Preferred shares typically carry additional rights to provide them with a certain level of control over the business and capital of the company – particularly so in venture capital transactions. These rights often include:
- Redemption rights (see *section 11 – Redemption*)
- Anti-Dilution (see *section 14 – Anti-Dilution*)
- Voting rights (see *section 19 – Voting Rights*)
- Drag-along provisions (see *section 28 – Drag-Along Right*)
- Co-sale provisions (see *section 27 – Co-Sale Right*)
- Rights of first refusal (see *section 26 – Rights of First Refusal*)

Preferred shares can be either *convertible* or *non-convertible*. Convertible preferred shares may be *simple convertible preferred shares* or *participating convertible preferred shares*. Non-convertible preferred shares give the investor the right to a preferred dividend or liquidation proceeds, making them more or less similar to subordinated debt securities. These shares have a limited upside potential for investors and are therefore rarely used in venture financings.

Simple convertible preferred shares provide the investor with an option to choose between a normal equity claim and a more debt-like claim, at the time of distribution of dividends (or liquidation proceeds). The investor has a normal equity claim if he converts his preferred shares into common shares. This enables the investor to share in the dividends on a pro rata basis with the other common shares. If, on the other hand, the investor does not convert his preferred shares, he retains his right to a preferred dividend and has a more debt-like claim. Simple convertible preferred shares provide both the upside potential of a common share, and the (limited) downside protection of a (non-convertible) preferred share.

Participating convertible preferred shares are the shares most used in venture capital financing. These shares combine the (limited) downside protection and the upside potential as discussed before, providing the holders thereof with both a debt-like claim and an equity claim. In the event of distribution of dividends, the holders of participating convertible preferred shares receive their preferred dividends first and thereafter participate on a pro rata basis with the common shares in the remaining dividends.

The features and rights that can be attached to preferred shares make this type of equity the ideal instrument for venture capital investors. The investors gain a certain level of control even while holding minority stakes in the company. Furthermore, it provides them with seniority over the holders of common shares when it comes to dividend payments and exit proceeds.

A venture-backed company usually issues several classes (or *series*) of preferred shares in its lifetime – one class for each investment round. The preferred shares issued in the most recent round have senior rights compared to the preferred shares issued in previous rounds (*junior preferred shares*). Distinguishing the rights enjoyed by different classes of preferred shares is common practice since the investments made at the time of the creation of each series are usually based on different valuations of the company and different circumstances, and consequently have different risk profiles.

Depending on the jurisdiction it may not be necessary to create shares that actually convert into shares of another class. In some jurisdictions the law provides the possibility to issue preferred shares that give preferential dividend rights in addition to the right to regular dividends on a pro rata basis with common shares.

B DEBT SECURITIES

I. GENERAL REMARKS

As opposed to equity, debt is a source of financing that does not entail ownership in a company. In the case of bankruptcy, unpaid debt is a liability of the company and therefore has priority over equity (which is not a liability of the company, but represents ownership). Using debt as an investment instrument therefore (in theory) reduces the investors' risks. In venture capital practice though, a bankrupt company will seldom be able to pay back any debt (let alone equity).

Since debt is not an ownership interest in the company, it does not have any upside potential other than the payment of interest. Consequently, debt limits investors' upside potential. Under ordinary circumstances, venture capital investors therefore prefer to target the (unlimited) potential of capital gains provided by the appreciation of their equity, rather than the (limited) interest payments and repayment of their investment.

II. BRIDGE LOANS

Even in the venture capital sector, in certain circumstances debt is a more logical financing instrument than equity. For example, if a company is in acute need of financing there will not be sufficient time to obtain such financing through a private placement or public offering. Sometimes a lack of time may not be the issue, but investors in a company may feel the time is not yet right to obtain financing through a new investment round. This could for example be the case if a company has not timely achieved certain milestones that are crucial to a good valuation, while the investors expect such milestones will be achieved if the company is given more time. In such a cases an interim solution is needed to pay for the company's operating expenses until new financing becomes available from a subsequent private placement or public offering. As an instrument of bridge financing, debt (a *bridge loan*) can provide such interim solution.

If the purpose of the bridge loan is to finance the company in the course of a public offering, the loan is typically repaid to the investors from the proceeds of the public offering. However, if a bridge loan is intended to *bridge the gap* between two private equity rounds, the loan will typically convert into equity issuable at the new financing round and on the same terms and valuation of such a financing round.

Bridge loans may have many different features, depending on the goals they serve. Typically, bridge loans are *short-term loans* (they come in terms of three to twelve month maturities) provided by existing shareholders seeking to safeguard their existing interest. They are normally repayable or convertible at maturity and, in general, are not callable prior to maturity. If on the date of maturity, the loan is not converted into shares and is not repaid, the company is in default, providing the investors with leverage in their negotiations to restructure the company's board and/or capital structure. In most cases, the investor will retain the right to convert to equity at a defined price if a deemed liquidation event (e.g. sale or merger of the company) occurs prior to the maturity date of the loan. This provides the investors with the benefits of an equity return, instead of repayment of the loan out of the proceeds of the deemed liquidation event. It is also not unusual that an exit triggers repayment of x times the principal amount (usually two times). Furthermore, a commonly used instrument to make it attractive for investors to provide a loan is warrant coverage (see *section 6 – Warrant Coverage*, of this chapter).

Bridge loans are normally provided in the form of a convertible loan agreement, which may include, amongst other things, covenants, representations and warranties from the company and its management.

As mentioned above, bridge loans typically convert into equity issuable at the new financing round and on the same terms and valuation of such a financing round. Using the terms and conditions of the new financing round has two advantages. Firstly, the existing investors can provide the bridge loan immediately without complicated negotiations regarding the share price and other terms. Secondly, the valuation of the company will be determined by the market (i.e. the new investors) and not by the existing investors, who would benefit from a low valuation. A new financing round is usually defined as (i) a financing round at a minimum valuation of the company of x; and/or (ii) a financing round with a minimum invested amount of y.

The financial risks involved with bridge loans can be considerable. The investors provide money to a company that has no more money, and does not (yet) have the capability to close a new financing round. Furthermore, the providers of a bridge loan run the risk that the new investors do not accept the bridge loan as a partial pre-payment of the new financing round. In such event the bridge loan can't convert into equity issuable at the new financing round, but will have to convert into a more junior (existing) type of equity. The new investors won't make their investment unless the bridge loan has been converted into such junior equity (a *pre-money conversion*). The price per share that the new investors will pay will be calculated on a fully diluted basis, including the shares issued upon conversion of the bridge loan. Obviously, the longer a bridge loan is outstanding before closing an equity round, the higher the risk that the bridge loan will be converted pre-money.

For taking on the risk of providing the bridge loan, the investors, or rather: the lenders, may feel that they are entitled to a "bonus". Usually this bonus will consist of a discount (where the bridge loan converts at discount of, say, 15-20% compared to the new money coming in) or warrant coverage (see *section 6 – Warrant Coverage,* of this chapter). Obviously, new investors will only be willing to invest in a new round if they feel the bonus is fair and reasonable and only dilutes the existing shareholders. A reward can also be structured by claiming a higher than usual interest rate. The unpaid interest can then be converted into shares in the same manner as the principal amount of the loan. If a bridge loan is provided by only a limited number of shareholders, then the other shareholders may view the terms of the bridge loan as too favourable for the lenders. Therefore, it is recommended to offer all shareholders the right to participate (on a pro rata basis and under the same terms and conditions) in the bridge financing. If a shareholder chooses not to participate, he will lose his right to object to these terms.

Originally, bridge loans were used to bridge a gap to the next financing round. They have however also become quite common in the seed phase of a company, before concrete plans for a financing round have been made. If used in seed financing, bridge loans are usually referred to as *convertible notes* or just *convertibles*. When used as seed funding it is common to agree on a valuation cap (maximum valuation). If the company's valuation at the new financing round is above the amount of the valuation cap, the loan will be converted at a conversion price based on the valuation cap. Thus, it determines the minimum number of shares that the investor will obtain at conversion. Be aware that a valuation cap can – unintendedly – serve as a maximum benchmark for investors in a new financing round.

Opting for a bridge loan in seed financing is typically considered a fast and cheap way to get a start-up funded. There is less need for lengthy discussions about legal terms, since bridge loans in seed financing are usually provided based on standard convertible loan agreements. Moreover, the discussion on the valuation of the company – which can be extremely difficult with very early stage start-ups – will be postponed until the next financing round.

A variation on convertibles notes is the SAFE – Simple Agreement for Future Equity – which is a convertible note without a maturity date. The SAFE was developed by the US seed accelerator *Y-combinator* and is commonly used in the US for seed financing instead of traditional convertible notes. Since the SAFE lacks a maturity date, it is arguably not a loan and could be considered a pre-payment on a capital investment.

Providing a convertible loan instead of equity may seem attractive from both the company's and investors' point of view. Investors should however keep in mind that the company will most likely not be able to pay back their money if no new financing round or exit takes place. The investment is at full risk from the moment it is provided, while conversion takes place at a future valuation. If the company is doing very well thanks to the convertible note investment, the noteholder will be "punished" by seeing the conversion price go up.

Negotiation tips:
- If there are various convertible note holders, try to "bundle" them and to provide the most essential rights, such as the right to demand repayment of the loan, not to each individual note holder, but to the meeting of note holders, usually called "the lenders' majority" instead.
- To execute a conversion, even in case of an 'automatic conversion', the company will need to take certain legal actions; e.g. to issue the shares. These steps should be carefully described in the loan documentation and agreed upon in advance by all shareholders in the company, so that the issue of shares will become an automated process.

Type of Security:	Series [●] convertible preferred shares (the "**Series [●] Shares**") are initially convertible on a 1:1 basis into the Company's common shares (the "**Common Shares**"). The Series [●] Shares and all other outstanding preferred shares (the "**Junior Preferred Shares**") are jointly referred to as the "**Preferred Shares**".

4.6 WARRANT COVERAGE

In compensation for making a debt or equity investment that the investors believe involves an unusual risk, investors may require the company to *sweeten* the deal by granting them warrants. A warrant is basically a call option – a right to buy a specified number of shares at a fixed exercise price by exercising said right prior to a specified expiration date. The period in which the warrants can be exercised (the *exercise period*) is typically three to five years. The number of shares that the investors are entitled to purchase, typically equals a certain percentage of the amount invested by such investor (the *warrant coverage*), divided by the exercise price of the warrant.

Example: If the investors in the Series A round make an aggregate investment of €8 million at a price per share of €9.38, and New Wave Energy grants a 25% warrant coverage, then the investors are entitled to purchase additional shares during the exercise period for an amount of €2 million. The number of shares that can be purchased if the exercise price is €9.38 amounts to 213,333 shares.

The exercise price of a warrant is normally equal to the price that is paid for the underlying share at the time of the warrant grant. The investors will therefore only benefit from the warrant if the company is able to increase its value during the exercise period. If the value of the underlying shares falls below the exercise price of the warrants, the investors will not exercise the warrant.

Warrants are exercisable by payment of the exercise price by the warrant holder. Sometimes however, warrants also have a 'cash-less' exercise feature, which allows the warrant holders to exercise their warrants without paying any cash.

The number of shares to which an investor is entitled if he opts for the cashless exercise of his warrants can be calculated using the following formula:

$$X = \frac{Y(A-B)}{A}$$

where **X** = the number of shares to be issued to the warrant holder if he opts for the cash-less exercise of the warrants;
Y = the number of shares purchasable under the warrant;
A = the fair market value of the share at the date of such calculation; and
B = the exercise price of the warrant.

Example: If in the previous example the Series A investors in New Wave Energy decide to exercise their warrants on a cash-less basis, and assuming that the fair market value of the underlying shares equals €12.50 per share, the warrant holder will be entitled to:

$$\frac{213{,}333\,(€12.50 - €9.38)}{€12.50} = 53.248 \text{ shares}$$

Since the fair market value for private companies is difficult to determine, the cash-less exercise feature typically applies to shares that have been listed on a stock exchange. The cash-less exercise can then be settled by a transfer agent or a broker. Nevertheless, investors may require that the warrants they hold in a private company can be exercised on a cash-less basis. The fair market value is then usually determined in good faith by the supervisory board or by an independent third party (e.g. an accountant).

Be aware that unexercised warrants may raise questions from potential investors when you want to raise a new investment round, distracting discussions from the more important topics. Therefore, try to avoid having unexercised warrants when raising a new investment round if at all possible. Also take into account the amount of legal paperwork involved in setting up a warrant scheme. A warrant scheme often comes in addition to a bridge loan agreement (or the issue of promissory notes). What is intended as a quick way to help the company through a few months and to reward the investors for their support, can become a 'lawyers' paradise'.

Warrant Coverage:	In addition to the Series [●] Shares, the Investors will also receive [___]% warrant coverage. For each Series [●] Share purchased, an Investor will receive a warrant to purchase [__] Common Shares/Series [●] Shares. The warrants will have a term expiring on the earlier of (i) [___] years from issuance or (ii) the date of completion of a Qualified Offering. The warrants will have standard anti-dilution protections. The warrants will be exercisable in cash or on a cash-less basis, at the option of the holder, at an exercise price of [Original Purchase Price] per share.

4.7 SHARE PRICE AND VALUATION

Valuation of non-listed companies can be a complex issue. It is often one of the most important issues in a venture capital transaction. The valuation process is usually associated with complex calculations and therefore thought of as an *exact science*. In reality though, the main drivers of the valuation process in venture capital transactions (especially in the case of less mature companies) have very little to do with exact science. Often the valuation is to a large extent based on subjective, rather than objective, variables. Issues such as the quality of the management team, the size and maturity of the market, the uniqueness of the technology, the stage of product development, the competitive landscape, the previous post-money valuation, the reputation of the investors in the company, etc. are extremely important factors for determining the value of a company.

In venture capital transactions, the value of the company, immediately prior to the investment is referred to as the *pre-money valuation*; while the value of the company, immediately after such investment is referred to as the *post-money valuation*. The *pre-money valuation* needs to be determined in order to set the share price for a proposed investment.

Although it may appear attractive for existing shareholders to set the pre-money valuation as high as possible, it is important to realise that doing so could give rise to problems at a later stage. If in the future the company needs to raise new capital, it will be difficult or maybe even impossible to do so if the value of the company has not increased since the last round, or worse: if it has decreased (in other words: in the case of a down round).

In such cases VCs will be reluctant to invest. Furthermore, founders and (key) employees with an equity stake in the company may become demotivated if anti-dilution provisions of the existing investors come into force (see section 14 – Anti-Dilution, of this chapter). Consequently, what appears to be attractive in the short run is not always attractive in the longer run.

The share price is calculated by dividing the pre-money valuation by the total of (i) the outstanding shares and (ii) any additional shares which may be issued due to the exercise of options, warrants, convertible debt or other rights to purchase shares in the company. The aforementioned sum is referred to as the *fully diluted* number of shares of the company.

To illustrate this we have added the cap table of *New Wave Energy* below (see section 3, of chapter 2):

	Pre financing		SERIES A			Post financing	
	Common Shares	% Holding	Amount €	Shares issued	Issuance ESOP	Total # Shares	% Holding
Bill Pear	600,000	38%				600,000	23%
Peter Singh	400,000	25%				400,000	16%
VC 1	600,000	38%	€2,000,000	213,333		813,333	32%
VC 2			€6,000,000	640,000		640,000	25%
ESOP					125,000	125,000	5%
Total	1,600,000	100%	€8,000,000	853,333	125,000	2,578,333	100%
Valuation	Pre-money		€15,000,000	Price per share		€9.38	
	Investment round		€8,000,000				
	Post-money		**€23,000,000**				

After closing of the Series A financing the share price of New Wave Energy is €8.92 on a fully diluted basis (€23,000,000 post-money valuation divided by 2,578,333 fully diluted outstanding shares), and €9.38 on a non-diluted basis (€23,000,000 post-money valuation divided by 2,453,333 actually outstanding shares (i.e. total shares less 125,000 options to purchase shares under the ESOP)).

Sometimes investors try to negotiate that the option pool comes out of the pre-money valuation, so the burden of the option pool is on the existing investors and founders only. Please refer to *section 30-Option Pool* of this chapter.

Valuation methods (such as discounted cash flow (DCF) analysis, and earnings or revenue multiples) that may be useful for mature companies are of little use for the valuation of an early stage company. The accuracy of a DCF valuation depends on the accuracy of the forecasts used for such a valuation. If the forecasts are not accurate, the valuation is worthless. Rather than applying these traditional methods, a venture capitalist will look at the post-money valuation as a matter of percentages. Let's assume only one investor will provide the required amount of financing. The investor has determined he is willing to invest that amount in the company, provided he obtains at least a certain percentage of the shares in the company. Usually this percentage varies from 25% to 40%, regardless of the amount of financing. The final percentage will, of course, be the result of negotiations between the investor and the existing shareholders. This final percentage combined with the amount of financing determines the post-money value of the company.

Example: *The required amount of financing of Company X is €3,000,000. VC1 is willing to invest this amount in exchange for 40% of the shares in Company X. If VC1 and Company X agree on this percentage, the post-money value of Company X will be €7,500,000 (€3,000,000 divided by 40%).*

Timing is crucial in negotiating a good valuation. If a company is running out of money at very short notice, the founders are standing with their backs against the wall and have no choice but to accept any valuation the investor comes up with. Therefore founders should take into account that raising money, from the first talks with potential investors until closing, generally takes at least four to six months.

Sometimes the founders' expectations regarding the company's valuation are too high and the investor and founders can't agree on a valuation. In such cases founders sometimes sweeten the high valuation by offering the investor liquidation preferences and other financial rights (such as anti-dilution protection). In practice however, this does not always work. Please refer to *section 14-Anti-Dilution* and *section 16-Liquidation Preference* of this chapter for a more extensive discussion of these matters. To bridge a gap between the investor's valuation and the valuation of the founders, valuation milestones can be a useful tool (see *section 3 – Milestones*, of this chapter). Reaching the stated milestones in the agreed timeframes then serves as a confirmation that the founders' valuation of the company was not too optimistic.

Share Price and Valuation: [Alternative 1: €[___] per share (the "Original **Purchase Price**") representing a fully diluted pre-money valuation of €[___].]

[Alternative 2: €[___] per share (the "**Original Purchase Price**"). The Original Purchase Price represents a fully diluted pre-money valuation of €[___] based on all outstanding Common Share equivalents, including options and warrants, at the time of the Closing and including (a) [___] new options as an increase to the option pool, as reflected in the capitalisation table attached as Appendix [___] and (b) the additional shares issuable to the holders of Junior Preferred Shares as a result of the anti-dilution protection in connection with the transaction contemplated in the Term Sheet.]

4.8 CAPITAL STRUCTURE

The term *capital structure* as used in the term sheet refers to an overview of the company's equity securities and, if any such securities have been issued, non-equity securities that can be converted into equity securities. Such an overview is typically provided in a capitalisation table or *cap table*, which is normally attached as an appendix to the term sheet but may also be included in the clause *Capital Structure* itself in an abbreviated version.

A complete cap table gives an overview of all securities issued and issuable (for example in connection with the exercise of options) by the company, their allocation (the identity of the holders of the securities), and the investments made in exchange for such securities. Together with the post-money valuation, the cap table will be the basis for the determination of the price per share, payable by the investors contemplating an investment and should give the fully diluted picture, including all options, warrants and securities convertible into shares.

Capital Structure:	The attached capitalisation table (Appendix [___]) details all of the securities that will be outstanding immediately prior to and after the Closing.

4.9 ANTICIPATED CLOSING DATE

The *closing date* is the date on which the investors will consummate the transaction, or in legal jargon, when the legal titles to the shares and to the funds are exchanged. After executing the term sheet, the investor will do due diligence and parties will negotiate a "subscription and shareholders agreement". The date of signing of the subscription and shareholders agreement is usually referred to as the *signing date*. The closing date does not necessarily need to coincide with the signing date, although from a practical point of view this is the preferred option. Sometimes the investor needs time between signing and closing to finalise legal formalities concerning the approval of the investment by the company's corporate bodies and/or by the regulatory authorities.

Before closing, the investors transfer the investment amount to an escrow account of the lawyer or notary public involved in the transaction, which will be released to the company at the closing date on fulfilment of all closing conditions. These conditions include the receipt by the company of the above-mentioned approvals but may also consist of other conditions to closing, like the absence of a material adverse change in the financial condition of the company. If the parties have agreed to a staged investment, a closing date will be agreed for each tranche.

The investor (or the lead investor) sets the anticipated closing date based on the company's information as available to the investors at the time of signing of the term sheet. This date is chosen to allow sufficient time to satisfy all conditions precedent such as the due diligence investigation and negotiation of the subscription and shareholders agreement (see *section 46 – Conditions Precedent,* of this chapter). The period required to close a venture deal usually varies from one to three months. It is in the interests of all parties to close the transaction as soon as practically possible. If a closing takes longer than necessary, the deal will lose momentum, the parties will tend to focus on less important matters and the deal may fall apart altogether. By linking the closing date to the exclusivity and no-shop clause (see *section 42 – Exclusivity/No-Shop,* of this chapter) and by agreeing to a short exclusivity period, the company can exert influence on the time frame of the closing process.

Anticipated Closing Date:	[date] (the "Closing"). [provide for multiple closings if applicable].

4.10 DIVIDENDS

A dividend is a portion of the earnings of a company that is distributed to the shareholders of the company. Usually the dividend amount depends on the profit made in the year to which the dividend pertains. Typically, dividends are declared by the annual meeting of shareholders, upon a proposal of the management board. Dividends can be paid in the form of a stock dividend or in cash.

One of the preferential rights that attaches to preferred shares in practically all cases is a dividend preference. This entitles the holder of preferred shares to receive dividends before the payment of dividends on the common shares. In most cases, preferred shares yield a fixed dividend based on the subscription price of the preferred share, just as debt yields an interest based on the principal loan amount. The dividend to be paid on preferred shares generally reflects a minimal IRR required by the investors. Rates of preferred dividend typically vary from 5% to 15%.

Dividends can be *participating* or *non-participating*. Non-participating dividends are most common and limit dividend distributions to the preferred shareholders to a fixed dividend amount or percentage. In the case of preferred shares with non-participating dividends, it is therefore possible that the dividends paid on common shares are higher than those paid on the preferred shares. Participating dividends allow the preferred shareholders to also have a share (on a share-for-share basis with the common shareholders) in the dividends available for distribution after the preferred dividend has been paid.

The investors' position can be further enhanced by determining that the preferred dividend will be cumulative. In such a case, if the company does not pay dividend, the amount of the preferred dividend will accumulate and has to be paid in full before dividends can be paid on the common shares. If, for example, a company misses two years of dividend payment, the holders of cumulative preferred shares will be entitled to repayment of all the missed preferred dividend amounts pertaining to those two years, before any dividends can be paid to the common shareholders. If dividends are non-cumulative, no such entitlement to repayment of missed amounts exists.

A dividend preference may seem pointless in many typical venture capital transactions. Why provide for a dividend preference in cases where it is clear the company will need all the cash it can get to fuel its growth? In the case of such high-growth, non-dividend-paying companies, a dividend preference may nevertheless be attractive to the investor, especially when such dividends are cumulative. By linking cumulative dividends to so-called liquidity events, the dividends on preferred shares function as a built-in return, accruing every year, resulting in an increase of the investors' claim to the proceeds of any sale of the company or redemption of their shares (see *section 16 – Liquidation Preference* and *section 11 – Redemption*, of this chapter).

Example: If VC1 invests €5,000,000 in the Series A round with a cumulative dividend of 10% and the company is sold two years later while no dividends have been paid by the company, VC1 will be entitled to €6,000,000 in liquidation preference (instead of the €5,000,000 VC1 would be entitled to if the dividend on the preferred shares were not cumulative). If the term sheet indicates that the cumulative dividend compounds annually (meaning that dividends will also be payable over unpaid dividends), VC1 will even be entitled to €6,050,000.

Negotiation tips:
- All distributions to the investors by way of dividend payments should be regarded as a pre-payment on the liquidation preference. In other words: if the dividend distributions result in the full repayment of the investors in accordance with the liquidation preference clause, the liquidation preference rights of the investors should automatically terminate. Make sure this is all clearly stated in the legal documents (this is not always the case).
- A high dividend rate may dilute the management's profit share significantly and can therefore be bad for their morale. New investors will be looking for the same or better terms, making the problem even bigger. Keep this in mind when determining the dividend rate.

Dividends: The Series [●] Shares will carry a dividend in preference to the Common Shares of [___]% of the Original Purchase Price per annum, which will accrue and cumulate annually and will be payable only if declared.

[The dividend will be payable in Series [●] Shares at the Original Purchase Price or in cash at the option of the Investors in the event of a liquidation or a Deemed Liquidation Event and without any compounding.]

[Without the approval of the holders of a [qualified] majority of the Series [●] Shares, no dividends will be paid on the Common Shares or Junior Preferred Shares so long as Series [●] Shares are outstanding.]

4.11 REDEMPTION

The term *redemption* refers to a repurchase of shares by the company. A redemption provision makes it possible for the investor to force the company to repurchase the investors' preferred shares. The redemption price is often equal to the liquidation preference, including accrued and unpaid dividends. However, other redemption prices are also used (e.g. a multiple of the liquidation preference, a fair market value notion, or the original purchase price plus a fixed annual percentage).

Obviously, the goal of every investor is to invest in companies that will become a great success, preferably sooner rather than later. Unfortunately, not every venture-backed company is assured of success. Some companies may go bankrupt. Others may only be a moderate success. In the latter case, the management of the company may be content to keep things going the way they were and may not actively pursue the creation of an exit for the investors.

The lack of active pursuit by the company's management of an exit constitutes a major problem for the investors. Many investors operate investment funds with a limited life span. These funds must be fully divested prior to their termination. One way or the other, they must be able to sell their investments. In many venture-backed companies, investors hold a minority shareholders' position, making it impossible to properly address the problem by dismissing or replacing the management without the consent of other shareholders. In such cases, the redemption clause may be the only instrument the investors have to solve their problem. It may offer them a way to get their investment back and receive some return in the form of accrued dividends.

A growing company is unlikely to have the cash required to meet the redemption. A more realistic scenario therefore is that the company will be unable to repay the investors when they call for the redemption of their shares. In such a scenario, the redemption clause will primarily function as an instrument to force the management to pursue an exit on a short notice. This may result in a forced sale of the company or (part of) its assets. The ultimate punishment will be that the investors will file for the bankruptcy of the company in case the company does not give full effect to the redemption. In that case, the investors may be able to recover some of their investment from the liquidation proceeds pursuant to their preferred liquidation rights. From the point of view of the company, mandatory redemption clauses are highly unattractive. Obviously, the exercise of a redemption clause may be the cause of a fierce clash between the entrepreneur and the investors.

While dealing with redemption clauses, careful attention should be paid to the limitations imposed by the applicable law. Under various jurisdictions procedural requirements and restrictions apply to the redemption of shares. These requirements were created to protect creditor's rights in the case of a repurchase of shares by the company. An alternative for a redemption clause – e.g. if redemption is not allowed due to restrictions under the applicable jurisdiction – is to have the founders grant the investor a *put option* under which the investor can sell his shares to the founders at a certain predetermined price after five to seven years. Thus, while not technically repurchasing the shares, a very similar effect can be achieved.

A redemption right normally does not apply until five to seven years after the initial investment date. However, all sorts of variations can be negotiated in redemption clauses. The redemption clause set out below includes two alternatives. One allows all shares to be redeemed at once, while the other provides for a phased redemption.

Redemption:	At the election of the holders of at least [___]% of the Series [●] Shares, subject to any restrictions under applicable law, the Company will redeem (...)
	[Alternative 1: (...) all outstanding Series [●] Shares in full, at any time after the fifth anniversary of the Closing.]
	[Alternative 2: (...) one third of the outstanding Series [●] Shares on the fourth anniversary, one half of the outstanding Series [●] Shares on the fifth anniversary of the Closing and all of the remaining outstanding Series [●] Shares on the sixth anniversary of the Closing.
	Such redemption will be at a purchase price equal to the Original Purchase Price (as adjusted for stock splits, stock dividends and the like) plus any accrued and unpaid dividends.
	In the event that the Company does not have funds legally available for such redemption, the Series [●] Shareholders will have the right to require the Company to take any further steps necessary to effect a sale of the Company, including retention of an investment banker appointed by the Series [●] Shareholders to actively market the Company for sale to a third party.]

4.12 VOLUNTARY CONVERSION

The voluntary conversion right permits a shareholder to convert his preferred shares into common shares and indicates how many common shares each preferred share will convert into (the *conversion ratio*). This is based on the assumption that parties have opted for a mechanism of conversion rates that will be adjusted if certain events occur. This may not always be the case. If it is not, other compensation mechanisms will be included, such as the issue of additional shares in case an anti-dilution provision is triggered.

If parties do opt (as we do in this book) for a mechanism of adjustable conversion rates, the conversion ratio can be determined by dividing the original purchase price of each preferred share by a 'conversion price'. Initially, this conversion price will be equal to the original purchase price and consequently the conversion ratio will be 1:1. Therefore, immediately after the issue of preferred shares each preferred share is convertible into one common share. However, under certain circumstances, the conversion price (and consequently the conversion ratio) may be adjusted.

One of the circumstances under which the conversion price may be adjusted is when the anti-dilution protection is triggered, provided that, in such a case, the mechanism for compensation under the anti-dilution clause foresees in an adjustment of the conversion rate instead of the immediate issue of shares.

Example: Let us assume the original purchase price of the preferred shares held by an investor is €5. Initially, the conversion price will be €5 as well. At a certain point in time, the company decides to double the number of its outstanding shares by issuing new shares. The value of the company has gone down. New shares will be issued at an issue price of €2.50. Consequently, the 'old' shares in the company will have lost 50% of their value. As a result, assuming full ratchet anti-dilution protection applies (see section 14 – Anti-dilution, of this chapter) the conversion price will be reduced from €5 to €2.50. This in turn will result in a conversion ratio of 2 (5 divided by 2.50). In other words, if the investor decides to voluntarily convert his preferred shares into common shares after the new shares have been issued; he will be entitled to twice as many common shares as before.

Since investors will lose all preferred rights attached to the preferred shares when they are converted, voluntary conversion would not be considered under normal circumstances. However, it can be an invaluable right if the investors hold non-participating preferred shares *(preferred shares that do not share in the proceeds of a liquidation or sale of the company after the investors have received the subscription price of their shares)*. In such a case, investors may be able to generate higher returns on their investment by converting their preferred shares into common shares (see *section 5 – Type of Security* and *section 16 – Liquidation Preference*, of this chapter).

In the event that the company increases the number of shares outstanding (and at the same time reduces the value of each share) by issuing stock dividends or effecting stock splits, the conversion price will be adjusted proportionally. Furthermore, when the investment is made subject to the achievement of milestones, adjustment of the conversion rate is often used as a mechanism to adjust the valuation when such milestone is not met (see *section 3 – Milestones,* of this chapter).

In the same manner, dividend that has accrued and has not yet been paid to the preferred shareholders may be convertible into common shares based on the applicable conversion price.

Voluntary Conversion:	A holder of Series [●] Shares will have the right to convert Series [●] Shares, or any part of such shares including declared dividends, at the option of the holder, at any time, into Common Shares. The total number of Common Shares into which each Series [●] Share may be converted will be determined by dividing the Original Purchase Price by the conversion price. The conversion price will initially be equal to the Original Purchase Price. The conversion price will however be subject to a proportional adjustment for share dividends, splits, combinations and similar events and in accordance with the 'Anti-Dilution' clause.
	[Milestone: the conversion price of the Series [●] Shares will be adjusted to €[___] per share if the Company fails to meet any of the milestones set forth in Appendix [___] to this Term Sheet.]

4.13 AUTOMATIC CONVERSION

The automatic conversion clause is aimed mainly at dealing with a possible initial public offering (IPO) of the company's shares. An IPO is an important event for investors as well as the company. An IPO can offer investors a good *exit opportunity* and can mark the beginning of an important new phase for the company. However, if the circumstances under which the IPO takes place are not carefully considered, the interests of the investors as well as those of the company could be jeopardised.

The purpose of the automatic conversion clause is to pre-establish the circumstances under which both the investors and the company agree an IPO should take place and to ensure that the company's capitalisation structure facilitates an IPO. In the latter issue, a company with different classes of shares and different rights attached to each class is not a very attractive IPO candidate. The market prefers simple capitalisation structures to complex ones. *Market investors* generally do not wish to invest in companies that have different classes of shares, especially if the classes that are not available to the public have much stronger rights than those available to the public. Consequently, the complex capitalisation structure of the company requires to be *cleaned up* immediately prior to an IPO. This clean-up is achieved by automatically converting all preferred shares into common shares in the case of an IPO that meets the pre-determined criteria.

Since the preferred shareholders will become common shareholders as a consequence of the conversion and lose all their preferred rights (e.g. rights facilitating alternative exit scenarios such as drag-along rights, co-sale rights, and redemption rights), the automatic conversion clauses usually contain two criteria that must be met in order for the IPO to be acceptable to the investors. The first criterion is that *the IPO should ensure a certain return on the investors' investment*. The second criterion is that *the IPO should generate a certain amount of proceeds for the company*. An IPO is a relatively expensive way to raise money. After deduction of the costs involved, the company should still have sufficient finances to achieve profitability, or value-creating milestones.

An important factor for consideration in this context is that the amount to be raised from the public, and the shares offered in exchange should be of sufficient substance to ensure a healthy liquidity in the company's publicly traded shares.

Consequently, automatic conversion clauses normally state that automatic conversion will occur if the IPO price per share is at least a certain multiple of the price per share originally paid by the investor, and the proceeds to the company equals a minimum pre-determined amount. The multiple and the amount of required proceeds will obviously differ for each transaction and will be determined in negotiations between the investors and the company. The longer it is expected to take a company to be ready for an IPO, the higher the multiple required by the investors will be.

In addition to ensuring automatic conversion upon a qualifying IPO, automatic conversion clauses usually contain a right for the holders of preferred shares to automatically convert all preferred shares to common shares if a qualified majority of (a class of) the preferred shares votes in favour of such a conversion. If an IPO does not qualify, the investors have room to negotiate with the company and the other shareholders before they agree to a conversion. Furthermore, this right enables (a majority of the) investors to push for an IPO pursuant to their demand right (see *section 21 – Registration Rights*, of this chapter) in cases where the requirements of a qualifying IPO are not met. In such cases, if a large enough majority of the shareholders is in favour of an IPO, they can force the company to go public (via the general shareholders' meeting). By utilising the aforementioned right, the qualified majority of the preferred shareholders can force a minority of the preferred shareholders that is not in favour of such an IPO, to convert its preferred shares into common shares and thus facilitate the IPO.

Automatic Conversion:	The Series [●] Shares, including declared dividends, and all other Preferred Shares will automatically be converted into Common Shares at the then applicable conversion price upon (i) the closing of a firmly underwritten public offering with a price per Common Share of at least [___] times the Original Purchase Price (subject to adjustments for share dividends, splits, combinations and similar events) and [net/gross] proceeds to the Company of not less than €[___] (a "Qualified Offering"), or (ii) upon the written consent of the holders of (a) [___]% of the Series [●] Shares, voting separately [and (b) [___]% of the Preferred Shares of the Company, voting together as a single class.

4.14 ANTI-DILUTION

Determining the valuation of a company is a complex issue. In early stage investments in particular, the valuation is, largely, the product of negotiations (see *section 7 – Share Price and Valuation*, of this chapter) and is sometimes proven wrong in a following investment round. Ideally, as a company develops, it increases its value, and thereby its share price. In a *down* round, however, the share price decreases, to less than the price paid by the investors in the previous round. To be protected against such economic (or price-based) dilution, investors require anti-dilution protection.

The *price-based anti-dilution* clause provides a protection mechanism that will be triggered whenever the company issues additional equity securities (shares or instruments convertible into shares) at a price that is lower than the price paid for the shares by the investors. Since the anti-dilution protection is an agreed right attached to the preferred shares, it serves as an advantage for the preferred shareholders (investors) over the common shareholders, who will pay the price for the dilution.

When anti-dilution protection is triggered, the protected investors obtain the right to receive additional shares. This right may be exercised either by adjusting the conversion ratio of the preferred shares into common shares, or by directly issuing additional shares to the investors. One of the advantages of the first mechanism (adjusting the conversion ratio) is that the investors do not have to pay for their additional shares. However, they will have to ensure that they can vote in the shareholders' meeting as if they had converted their preferred shares into common shares. In many European jurisdictions, voting rights are attached to the nominal value of the shares, often making voting on an 'as if converted' basis difficult (see *section 19 – Voting Rights*, of this chapter). Under the second mechanism (direct issue of shares), the investors may be obliged under the applicable law to pay a certain price for the shares (e.g. *the nominal value*) – potentially a considerable amount if a large number of new shares are issued. Under such a mechanism, the investors will naturally be entitled to the voting rights attached to the additional shares. Investors in the US will, without exception, use the first mechanism.

If the system of adjustable conversion rates is the preferred compensation mechanism, the anti-dilution provision could be drafted as follows:

"In the event that the Company issues new shares, or securities convertible into or exchangeable for shares, at a purchase price lower than the applicable conversion price of the Series [●] Shares, then the conversion price of the Series [●] Shares will be subject to a [full-ratchet/weighted average] adjustment (...)"

If additional shares are to be issued to the investors as the preferred compensation mechanism, the anti-dilution provision could read as follows:

"In the event that the Company issues new shares, or securities convertible into or exchangeable for shares, at a purchase price lower than the applicable purchase price of the Series [●] Shares, the holders of Series [●] Shares may elect that the Company shall procure (to the extent that it is lawfully able to do so) the issue to the holders of Series [●] Shares, of additional Series [●] Shares against payment of such an amount that the average purchase price they have paid is equal to the purchase price at which the new shares are issued."

There are two basic types of price-based anti-dilution protection: (a) *full ratchet anti-dilution protection* and (b) *weighted average anti-dilution protection*. The difference lies in the level of compensation available to the investors. We will discuss these types of protection below, based on the assumption that parties have agreed on the conversion adjustment as compensation mechanism.

A FULL RATCHET PROTECTION

The *full ratchet anti-dilution protection* is the most investor-friendly type of protection. Under the full ratchet protection, the investors will be put in the position as if they had invested at the new, lower issue price. This completely preserves the value of their initial investment in a down round. In the term sheet submitted to *New Wave Energy*, the anti-dilution clause indicates that a full ratchet adjustment will apply if *New Wave Energy* issues new shares at a price less than the applicable conversion price of the Series A Shares. A more extensive full ratchet clause, explaining the extent of the protection, could be drafted as follows:

"In the event that the Company issues equity securities at a purchase price less than the applicable conversion price of the Series A Shares, then the conversion price of the Series A Shares will be subject to a full ratchet adjustment, reducing the applicable conversion price of the Series A Shares to the price at which the new equity securities are issued."

The principle of the full ratchet protection can be illustrated by the following example.

Example: A Company has raised a Series A round at €2 per share and raises a subsequent Series B round at €1 per share. Under the full ratchet protection, the holders of Series A shares will be put in the position as if they had purchased the Series A shares at €1 per share instead of €2 per share, thus entitling them to twice the number of shares they held before the Series B round.

The full ratchet protection focuses on the new price per share and compensates the investors for the full difference in share price, regardless of the real impact of the dilutive event. Consequently, as per the example, the compensation for the holders of Series A shares will be the same regardless of whether the company issues only 1 new Series B share or 1 million new Series B shares. This can cause significant dilution of the value of the shares held by the shareholders that are not protected against price-based dilution (typically the common shareholders, i.e. founders and employees). The effects of a (full ratchet) anti-dilution protection may be perceived by those shareholders as a severe injustice and may have a demoralising effect on them. Companies that are in a position to negotiate better terms will try to have the investors settle for a less onerous form of anti-dilution protection, such as the weighted average anti-dilution protection.

B **WEIGHTED AVERAGE PROTECTION**
In contrast to the full ratchet protection, the *weighted average anti-dilution protection* takes into account the proportional relevance of the subscription price paid in the down round and the subscription price paid in the previous round. As in the full ratchet mechanism, it takes a new share price based on which the investors will be compensated. However, it will not bring the old price down to the new price of the down round, but will 'ratchet it down' to a new price (*weighted average price*) determined by the average of both prices, after they are weighted. For the new price, the weighting factor is the number of shares issued in the dilutive financing round. For the old price, the factor is either (i) the total number of common shares outstanding prior to the dilutive financing round on an 'as-if converted and fully diluted' basis – (*broad based weighted average*) or (ii) part of the shares outstanding prior to the dilutive financing round as specified in the term sheet (*narrow based weighted average*).

It is important to note that the *narrow based weighted average* basically stands for all weighted average calculations using less than the shares mentioned under (i) (*broad based weighted average*) as a weighting factor for the old price. Thus, in practice, the number of shares mentioned under (ii) can vary from all pre-money outstanding shares (on a non-converted and non-diluted basis) to only the preferred shares issued in the previous round. The narrower the base, the larger the effect of the new price and the more favourable the clause is to the protected investors.

To calculate the weighted average price, parties include a mathematical formula in their shareholders' agreement. Though each formula may look alike, the definition of Q1 may strongly vary. As explained above, protection based on either of the two averages depends on the definition of this symbol.

$$\text{Weighted Average Price} = \frac{P_1 Q_1 + P_2 Q_2}{Q_1 + Q_2}$$

where P_1 = the subscription price in the previous round[1];
P_2 = the subscription price in the new round;
Q_1 = broad based: the total number of shares outstanding prior to the dilutive financing round, on an 'as-if converted and fully diluted' basis;
'narrow based': part of the shares outstanding prior to the dilutive financing round as specified in the term sheet;
Q_2 = the number of shares issued in the new round.

A term sheet normally simply states that a weighted average protection is applicable, without including a formula or indicating whether a *broad based* or *narrow based* weighted average is to be applied. In view of the different levels of anti-dilution protection provided by each particular weighted average formula, the formula and its contents should ideally be a part of the discussion during the term sheet negotiations.

C COMBINATIONS AND OTHER FEATURES

Though not seen very often, the following modifications may be made to the full ratchet and the weighted average anti-dilution protections, to address specific needs or concerns of the investors or to find a solution to a deadlock situation. For instance, the concerned parties may agree to

---

[1] P_1 can also be defined as the "old conversion price" if the anti-dilution mechanism foresees an adjustment of the conversion ratio (see *section 14 – Anti-Dilution*, of this chapter). In such an event, "Weighted Average Price" should be read as "New Conversion Price".

calculate the compensation based on the average of the full ratchet and weighted average price. The formula is fairly simple:

$$X = \frac{FR + WA}{2}$$

where **X** = the actual number of additional (anti-dilution) shares to be issued to the investors;
FR = (full ratchet) number of additional shares to be issued under the full ratchet calculation;
WA = (weighted average) number of additional shares to be issued under the weighted average calculation.

Another alternative is to place a time limit on the full ratchet anti-dilution right, i.e. after a certain period, the full ratchet anti-dilution protection switches to a weighted average formula or is forfeited altogether. The following clause contains such a limitation:

"In the event that the Company issues equity securities prior to [date] at a purchase price less than the applicable conversion/subscription price of the Series [●] Shares, then the conversion price of the Series [●]Shares will be subject to a [full ratchet] [weighted average] adjustment."

A share price floor may also be included. If the new share price in the down round falls below a specific price, the full ratchet protection switches to a weighted average anti-dilution protection. An example of such a clause in a term sheet is the following:

"In the event that the Company issues equity securities at a purchase price (the **"Purchase Price"**) *less than the applicable conversion price of the Series [●] Shares, then the conversion/subscription price of the Series [●] Shares will be subject to: (i) a full ratchet adjustment, if the Purchase Price is greater than €[___] per share; and (ii) a weighted average adjustment if the Purchase Price is less than €[___] per share."*

Instead of using the down round alone as reference for the anti-dilution compensation, parties may include future rounds in the calculation of the dilution. The full ratchet or weighted average protection is then based on a new price calculated as the weighted average price of all future rounds.

This will limit the dilution when one *down* round is followed by *up* rounds. An example clause:

*"In the event that the Company issues equity securities in one or more issuances and if the weighted average of the purchase prices of such issuance or issuances (the **"Weighted Average Price"**) is less than the applicable conversion/subscription price of the Series [●] Shares, then the conversion price of the Series [●] Shares will be adjusted to the Weighted Average Price."*

In exchange for allowing the investors protection against future down rounds, the founders may negotiate a *pay-to-play* clause requiring the investors to invest their pro rata share in such rounds in order to retain their anti-dilution protection. Also, refer *to section 15 – Pay-to-Play* of this chapter.

D CARVE-OUTS AND ADJUSTMENTS

Not every issuance of shares under the original purchase price however, should trigger the anti-dilution protection. The most obvious exception is the issue of common shares upon conversion of the preferred shares. Another typical exception set out in term sheets is the issue of shares or options at a discount to employees under an employee stock option plan (ESOP).

Other, less obvious carve-outs should be judged by the investors or the Supervisory Board on the basis of individual cases. Examples are: common shares issued or issuable in connection with:

i. a merger or acquisition of the Company;
ii. any borrowings from a commercial lending institution;
iii. a public offering before or in connection with which all outstanding preferred shares will be converted to common shares or upon exercise of warrants or rights granted to underwriters in connection with such a public offering.

E CALCULATION PROBLEMS

Calculation of the new conversion price or the number of shares to be issued pursuant to the anti-dilution protection appears simple. In practice however, it can be quite complex. This is mainly because the anti-dilution protection is based on the share price in the new (down) round. The new share price is determined on a fully diluted basis, including all shares to be issued to the existing preferred shareholders pursuant to the anti-dilution protection. This results in a circular logic, which can be illustrated in the following example.

Example: New Wave Energy's post-money valuation after its Series A round is €23 million, based on 2,578,333 post-money shares outstanding (and a price per Series A share of €9.38). Let us assume that the Series B round is a down round and that the Series B investors value New Wave Energy at €15 million pre-money (note: pre-Series B round). Based on the 2,578,333 shares outstanding (pre-money fully diluted), the share price of a Series B share would be €5.82. However, the anti-dilution protection of the holders of Series A shares will increase the fully diluted outstanding shares pre-Series B, and will consequently decrease the share price. The decreased share price will trigger the anti-dilution price again, and so on.

F DILUTION OF OWNERSHIP

A distinction must be made between the concept of economic or *price-based dilution* as explained above and the *dilution of ownership*.

Dilution of ownership of the existing shareholders' percentage of the company's share capital occurs for example if the company issues additional shares to new shareholders. In such a situation, the pie has been divided into more – and therefore smaller – pieces. Dilution of ownership can be prevented by purchasing a proportional number of shares of any future issue of shares. A right to purchase such proportional number of shares is called a *pre-emptive right* (see *section 25 – Pre-Emptive Right*, of this chapter).

> **Negotiation tips:**
> - An anti-dilution clause should protect the old investors against price dilution in cases where new investors value the company at less than the last post-money valuation. In practice, however, new investors typically don't start price negotiations if they think the last post-money valuation was too high. In this situation, anti-dilution protection is ineffective and offers poor compensation for paying a (too) high price (due to a too high valuation).
> - It could be argued that anti-dilution protection in case of a down round should only be provided when outside investors join as shareholders and set the price. Only their valuation can be considered as the new company value in the 'market'.

Anti-Dilution: In the event that the Company issues new shares, or securities convertible into or exchangeable for shares, at a purchase price lower than the applicable conversion price of the Series [●] Shares, then the conversion price of the Series [●] Shares will be subject to a(n) (...)

[Alternative 1: (...) full ratchet adjustment, reducing the applicable conversion price of the Series [●] Shares to the price at which the new shares are (to be) issued.]

[Alternative 2: (...) [broad based][narrow based] weighted average adjustment, reducing the applicable conversion price of the Series [●] Shares to a new conversion price calculated in accordance with a weighted average anti-dilution formula.]

[Alternative 3: (...) full ratchet adjustment within [___] years of the Closing. Thereafter, the conversion price will be subject to adjustment on a [broad based][narrow based] weighted-average basis.]

[*Alternative 4*: (...) (a) [broad based][narrow based] weighted-average adjustment if the purchase price per share is equal to or greater than €[___] per share and (b) full ratchet adjustment if the purchase price per share is lower than €[___] per share.]

[*Alternative 5*: (...) adjustment, reducing the applicable conversion price of the Series [●] Shares to a new conversion price calculated as the average of the conversion prices resulting from the weighted average adjustment and the full ratchet adjustment (new conversion price = (WA + FR)/2).]

In the event that the Company issues new shares, or securities convertible into or exchangeable for shares, at a purchase price lower than the applicable purchase price of the Series [●] Shares, the holders of Series [●] Shares may elect that the Company shall procure (to the extent that it is lawfully able to do so) the issue to the holders of Series [●] Shares, additional Series [●] Shares against payment of such an amount that the average purchase price they have paid is equal to the purchase price at which the new shares are issued.

The anti-dilution adjustment will not apply in the event of issuance of (...)

[*Alternative 1*: (...) Common Shares issued or issuable to employees, consultants or directors of the Company directly or pursuant to the ESOP (as set out in the 'Employee Pool' clause) that have been approved by the Supervisory Board.].

[*Alternative 2:* (...) (i) Common Shares issued or issuable to employees, consultants or directors of the Company directly or pursuant to the ESOP (as set out in the 'Employee Pool' clause) that have been approved by the Supervisory Board; (ii) Common Shares issued or issuable upon conversion of the Preferred Shares; (iii) Common Shares issued or issuable in connection with a merger, acquisition, combination, consolidation or other reorganisation involving the Company and approved by the Supervisory Board of the Company; (iv) Common Shares issued or issuable in connection with (a) any borrowings from a commercial lending institution, (b) the lease of equipment or property by the Company, or (c) strategic partnerships and/or licensing relationships, so long as such transactions are approved by the Supervisory Board; and (v) Common Shares issued or issuable (a) in a public offering before or in connection with which all outstanding Preferred Shares will be converted to Common Shares or (b) upon exercise of warrants or rights granted to underwriters in connection with such a public offering.]

4.15 PAY-TO-PLAY

A *pay-to-play* clause is aimed at penalising investors who do not participate on a pro rata basis in a financing round, by cancelling some or all of their preferential rights.

The idea behind a pay-to-play clause is that the threat of losing these preferential rights will encourage investors to make additional investments in the company in cases where the valuation has been adjusted downward. Furthermore, this clause will prevent those investors who do *not* make additional investments from *free riding*. Such free riding would occur if investors, who do not make additional investments, were to retain all their preferential rights and, as a consequence of the dilutive effect of the down round, be entitled to additional shares under their anti-dilution protection.

The pay-to-play clause typically only applies to future (down) rounds. It is possible, however, that new investors in a down round are only prepared to invest in the company if the pay-to-play clause also applies to the down round in which they plan to make their first investment. In such cases, the pay-to-play clause can be drafted in such a manner that it also applies to investors who made their investment in a previous round. This will force these *old* investors to participate in the new (down) round and will prevent the founders from being diluted due to the investors' anti-dilution protection.

The most onerous version of *pay-to-play* is the automatic conversion into common shares, which essentially ends any preferential right of an investor, such as his liquidation preference, anti-dilution rights and control rights. A less onerous version is the automatic conversion into a new series of preferred shares, which is identical to the existing series but which may not have: (i) anti-dilution protection (or may have less favourable anti-dilution protection), (ii) liquidation preference, (iii) special voting rights, or (iv) a combination of the above. The forfeiture of rights under the pay-to-play clause is generally proportionate to the extent that the investor fails to participate in the new round.

Though it seems appropriate to make the non-participating investors pay for their unwillingness to play, not all investors are keen on implementing this clause at the time of their investment. After all, no investor can be entirely sure that he will (be able to) participate in a future investment round (on a pro rata basis). Since the pay-to-play clause prevents them from being diluted under investors' anti-dilution clauses, the founders and all other common shareholders are the main beneficiaries of this clause. For them, the pay-to-play clause can be a valuable tool in the term sheet negotiations.

Pay-to-Play: Holders of Preferred Shares are required to participate in any dilutive issuance [including the Series [●] Financing] to the extent of their pro rata equity interest in the Preferred Shares, [unless the participation requirement is waived for all Preferred Shareholders by the Supervisory Board [(including the Series [●] Director)]][unless the holders of [●]% of the Series [●] Shares elect otherwise].

In the event that a holder of Preferred Shares fails to participate in accordance with the previous paragraph, the Preferred Shares held by such shareholder will automatically [and proportionally], [lose their anti-dilution rights][lose their liquidation rights][convert to Common Shares].

4.16 LIQUIDATION PREFERENCE

The *liquidation preference* clause specifies how much of the proceeds of a liquidation the preferred shareholders can collect before any of these proceeds are distributed to the holders of common shares. If more series (classes) of preferred shares are outstanding, it will also describe in which order the holders of different series of preferred shares will be paid. Usually, the holders of preferred shares issued in the last round of financing rank *senior* or *ahead* of the holders of preferred shares issued in earlier rounds and the holders of common shares.

A LIQUIDATION EVENTS

As the term indicates, a liquidation preference is primarily applicable in the event of a liquidation, bankruptcy, dissolution, or winding up of a company. The liquidation preference allows the investors to recover certain amounts from the liquidation proceeds (if any) before all others. In certain circumstances, it may result in the investors recovering amounts, while the other shareholders do not receive any proceeds at all. A liquidation preference can thus provide investors with a certain degree of protection against their *downside* risk, at the cost of the other shareholders. However, due to the nature of equity, this protection is limited. In bankruptcy situations there are usually no proceeds at all to distribute among equity holders, since all debt must be repaid first.

Typically, the applicability of the liquidation preference is also extended to certain events other than liquidation or bankruptcy, such as the sale or merger of the company. These events are then deemed to be a liquidation event for purposes of allocating the distribution of the proceeds. By including these *deemed liquidation events* in the liquidation preference clause, preferred shares will provide the investors with additional coverage in case the company is not liquidated but sold to (or merged with) another company at a very low valuation (a *'fire sale'*). Moreover, provided that the investors have a participating liquidation preference (i.e. they hold *participating preferred shares* that entitle them to a pre-determined portion of the liquidation proceeds *and* to a pro rata part of the remainder of the proceeds shared with the common shareholders), they will, in addition to the aforementioned downside protection, obtain upside potential in the event of a (successful) sale or merger of the company.

The events that are to be considered a deemed liquidation under a liquidation preference clause often also include events like a reorganisation or a consolidation of the company, or the sale, lease, transfer or other disposition of all or substantially all of the company's assets. To qualify as a deemed liquidation event, these events must typically result in a loss of voting rights by the current shareholders (change of control).

Sometimes investors argue that an IPO should also trigger a liquidation event. This is undesirable, for two reasons. Firstly, an IPO should be regarded as an investment round rather than as a deemed liquidation event (e.g. the sale of the company). There are no distributable proceeds resulting from an IPO; the company merely issues new shares which are sold to 'the public' in order to raise new money. Like any investment round, an IPO should therefore not be subject to a liquidation preference arrangement. Secondly, immediately prior to the IPO all preferred shares will be converted into common shares (only common shares can be traded at a stock exchange). This conversion results in the loss of the liquidation preference that is attached to the preferred shares. The preferred shares will automatically convert in the event of a Qualified Offering (*see section 13 – Automatic Conversion*, of this chapter). An IPO can therefore not trigger the liquidation preference because no preferred shares will be outstanding at the time the company is actually listed at a stock exchange.

It should be noted that a distribution to the shareholders as a result of a winding up or bankruptcy of the company is an entirely different legal concept from the re-allocation of the sale price of the shares amongst the shareholders in case of a sale or merger of the company. The specific legal basis of each liquidation event, the specific document in which it is to be set forth (articles of association or shareholders' agreement), and the parties that need to agree to the liquidation preference are elements that should be carefully considered while drafting this clause in the term sheet and in the final documentation.

B TYPES OF LIQUIDATION PREFERENCE

In the previous section we have elaborated on the events that can trigger the liquidation preference. Now we will look into the different types of liquidation preference and their consequences for the holders of common and preferred shares. Liquidation preference clauses can be found in two basic forms: (i) a *non-participating liquidation preference* and (ii) a *participating liquidation preference*, each form depending on the type of convertible preferred shares used, and providing the investors with a different level of return. A third type of liquidation preference can be created by capping the participating liquidation preference.

I. NON-PARTICIPATING LIQUIDATION PREFERENCE

The most basic form of liquidation preference is the *non-participating liquidation preference* (also called: simple liquidation preference). This liquidation preference entitles only the holders of the (non-participating) preferred shares to a pre-determined portion of the liquidation proceeds, usually equivalent to the amount paid by them for the preferred shares. Under a non-participating liquidation preference, the preferred shareholders stop sharing in the proceeds after repayment of such amount. In circumstances where the proceeds exceed the preferred return of the investors, this may have the undesirable effect for the investors that they are not able to share in the upside. Therefore, this type of liquidation preference should always be read in conjunction with the ability of the holders of the preferred shares to convert their shares into common shares, as explained in more detail in *section 12 – Voluntary Conversion*, of this chapter. If however, under the applicable jurisdiction, a liquidation preference can be stipulated in such a way that it allows the preferred shareholders to choose between receiving either (i) their subscription price or (ii) the amount they would have received if they had converted the preferred shares to common shares, the need for conversion will not arise.

The non-participating liquidation preference can be increased by a multiple (e.g. 2x, 3x or more) or a dividend as explained in paragraph (iv) below.

The question of whether or not to convert in the case of a non-participating liquidation preference is illustrated in the following example.

Example: Let us assume that a venture-backed company has a share capital consisting of 50% common shares and 50% preferred shares. All preferred shares are held by one investor, who has invested €10 million in the company. The holder of preferred shares (the investor) is entitled to a 1x non-participating liquidation preference. Depending on the amount of proceeds available for distribution or reallocation, the investor will decide to claim his liquidation preference (€10 million) or his pro rata share of the liquidation proceeds (50%). His pro rata entitlement to the proceeds equals the investment amount (€10 million) when the proceeds of the liquidation are €20 million (€10/50%).

If the proceeds are less than €20 million, the investor will not convert since he will be better off with the liquidation preference. If the proceeds are more, he will definitely convert his preferred shares into common shares prior to distribution.

FIGURE 14: LIQUIDATION PREFERENCE 1X NON-PARTICIPATING

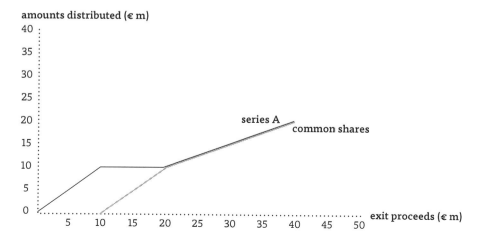

It should be noted that under this 1x simple liquidation preference there is a misalignment of interest between the holders of common shares and preferred shares for exit values between €0 and €20 million; the common shareholders will receive nothing if the proceeds are less than €10 million, while the holder of preferred shares won't benefit from any exit proceeds between €10 million and €20 million. We call the range of exit values between €0 and €20 million the 'zone of misalignment'. Investors tend to focus on the zone where they are indifferent or misaligned with the founders and call the range of exit values between €10 and €20 million (instead of the full range between €0 and €20 million) the 'zone of indifference' or 'dead zone'. As will be shown in the next paragraphs, the significance of such a zone will increase if terms become harsher.

II. PARTICIPATING LIQUIDATION PREFERENCE

The other basic type of liquidation preference is the *participating liquidation preference*. This type of liquidation preference entitles the holders of preferred shares to first receive the original purchase price of their preferred shares (the liquidation preference) and subsequently to share in the remaining proceeds as if their preferred shares had been converted into common shares immediately prior to the (deemed) liquidation event. This distribution principle offers a protection which is similar to the simple liquidation preference, but has an increased upside potential since the preferred shares will also share in the remaining proceeds, after the repayment of their investment. This double repayment feature attached to the participating preferred shares is often referred to as a *double dip*.

Example: Following up on the previous example, let's assume that the venture-backed company is sold for €25 million. If the investor (holder of preferred shares) has negotiated a 1x participating liquidation preference, he will receive first €10 million back based on his liquidation preference and will subsequently receive €7.5 million (50% of the remaining €15 million), bringing his total to €17.5 million. In the case of a non-participating liquidation preference, the investor would only have received €12.5 million.

FIGURE 15: LIQUIDATION PREFERENCE 1X PARTICIPATING

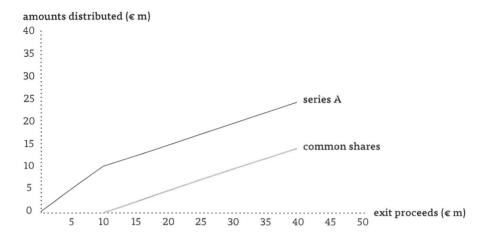

As illustrated in the above chart, only after the first €10 million has been distributed (to the holder of preferred shares) will the holder of common shares start sharing in the remaining proceeds. The zone of misalignment lies between the exit values of €0 and €10 million. However, it should be noted that misalignment continues to exist between the holders of preferred and common shares because the initial distribution to the holder of preferred shares is never 'caught up' by the holder of common shares.

III. CAPPED PARTICIPATING LIQUIDATION PREFERENCE

A common way to limit the dilutive effects of a participating liquidation preference is to impose a cap on the participation of the investor (holder of preferred shares) in the remaining proceeds. The holder of capped participating preferred shares will receive all the benefits of the participating preferred shares as mentioned above, but the total return is capped. Such a cap is typically fixed as a multiple of the original investment, such as 2x or 3x[2]. Once the investor has reached that cap, it will no longer share in the remaining proceeds. As a result, in circumstances where the investor's pro rata share in the total proceeds would yield a higher return than his preference and participation cap allows, the investor is forced to forego

---

2   Don't mistake this multiple for the multiple on liquidation preference explained under paragraph (iv), which has the opposite effect.

his preference and simply participate on an as-converted basis pro rata parte with the holder of common shares.

Example: *If the investor (holder of preferred shares) has negotiated a 1x participating liquidation preference which is capped at 2x, he will be entitled to receive an amount equal to 1x liquidation preference plus a pro rata distribution with the common shares until the total amount equals 2x his investment (€20 million). Since the investor in the above example owns 50% of the shares on a pro rata basis, he will only convert his preferred shares into common shares (in order to share in the proceeds on a pro rata basis) if the exit value exceeds €40 million.*

FIGURE 16: LIQUIDATION PREFERENCE 1X PARTICIPATING, 2X CAP

As shown in the above chart, the zone of misalignment is between €0 and €10 million and between €30 and €40 million.

IV. DIVIDENDS AND MULTIPLES

Irrespective of the fact that a *participating liquidation preference* is more investor friendly than a *non-participating liquidation preference*, market conditions sometimes impel investors to seek even better rights. The liquidation preference, whether simple or participating, can be improved for the investors by increasing the preferred repayment amount with *accrued and unpaid dividends* or by applying *multiple pay-out instruments*.

By increasing the liquidation preference with the amount of accrued and unpaid cumulative dividends, investors can increase their return on investment in the case of a liquidation event (see *section 10 – Dividends*, of this chapter). The same result may be achieved by using non-cumulative dividends, but obviously to a lesser extent.

Investors with sufficient leverage may negotiate multiple pay-out instruments. Under those circumstances, they will be paid out a certain multiple of the original purchase price before the remaining proceeds are distributed. The multiples vary from two to three times the investment amount in a certain *round*. In the event of a multiple of 2 (also referred to as a '2x' liquidation preference) in combination with an increase by accrued and unpaid dividends, the following wording may be used:

"(...) the holders of preferred shares will be entitled to receive, in preference to the holders of common shares, 2 (two) times the aggregate of the original purchase price plus any accrued and unpaid dividends."

Evidently, by combining cumulative dividends with a multiple pay-out instrument and the use of participating preferred shares, the investors will have the most favourable type of liquidation preference.

Early stage investors may shoot themselves in the foot by negotiating investor friendly liquidation preferences. Investors who invest in later rounds usually will require at least the same liquidation rights. They will also want their preferred shares to rank *senior* or *ahead* of the early investors. This can result in a situation where the holders of preferred shares issued in the last round of financing get everything and the early investors get nothing, despite their severe liquidation rights.

Liquidation Preference:	*In the event of a liquidation or winding up of the Company, the holders of Series [●] Shares will be* entitled to receive in preference to the holders of Junior Preferred Shares and the holders of Common Shares payment of an amount equal to [___ times] the Original Purchase Price per Series [●] Share [plus any accumulated and unpaid dividends].

If there are insufficient assets or proceeds to pay such amount to the holders of Series [●] Shares in full, the amount available will be paid on a pro rata basis between the holders of Series [●] Shares.

Thereafter, the holders of Junior Preferred Shares will receive payment in full of the original purchase price paid per Junior Preferred Share [plus any accumulated and unpaid dividends].

[Alternative 1: (non-participating liquidation preference): Thereafter, any remaining assets or proceeds will be paid exclusively to the holders of Common Shares on a pro rata basis.]

[Alternative 2: (participating liquidation preference): Thereafter, any remaining assets or proceeds will be distributed pro rata among the holders of Common Shares and the holders of Preferred Shares (the latter on an as-if converted basis).]

[Alternative 3: (non-participating with conversion at the option of investor): In the event of a liquidation (...), the holders of Series [●] Shares will be entitled to receive, in preference to the holders of common shares, an amount equal to the greater of (i) the Original Subscription Price of the Series [●] Shares held plus any accrued and unpaid dividends and (ii) the amount they would have received had they converted the Series [●] Shares to common shares immediately prior to such liquidation or winding up.]

[Alternative 4: (capped participating liquidation preference): Thereafter, any remaining assets or proceeds will be distributed pro rata among the holders of Common Shares and the holders of Preferred Shares (the latter on an as-if converted basis) until such time that the holders of Series [●] Preferred Shares have received an aggregate of [___ times] the Original Purchase Price per share (including any amounts paid pursuant to the paragraphs above). The balance thereafter will be distributed amongst the holders of Common Shares on a pro rata basis.]

A reorganisation, consolidation, merger of the Company, sale or issue of Shares or any other event pursuant to which the shareholders of the Company will have less than 51% of the voting power of the surviving or acquiring corporation, or the sale, lease, transfer or other disposition of all or substantially all of the Company's assets will be deemed to be a liquidation or winding up for the purposes of the liquidation preference (a **"Deemed Liquidation Event"**), thereby triggering the liquidation preferences described above [unless the holders of [___]% of the Series [●] Shares elect otherwise].

4.17 FAVOURABLE TERMS

Not only do venture capital term sheets summarise the basic terms and conditions under which a potential investment will be made, they also set out the basic structure of the transaction, the timelines for due diligence and the deadline for the closing. The purpose of a term sheet is to ensure that this exercise is done at an early stage of the investment process. At that time, the investors normally would not have had the opportunity to conduct a due diligence investigation or to otherwise review the existing rights, preferences and restrictions of the outstanding shares of the company.

As a general rule, investors in each round of financing will negotiate investment terms reflecting the investment risk they perceive, but they will in no event accept terms that are less favourable than the terms negotiated in earlier rounds. A *'Favourable Terms'* clause ensures that the rights attached to the shares to be issued to the investors in the new round will be equivalent to or better than those attached to the existing (preferred and common) shares.

Favourable Terms:	The terms herein, other than valuation, are subject to a review of the rights, preferences and restrictions pertaining to the existing shares in the Company. Any changes necessary to conform such existing shares to this Term Sheet will be made at the Closing as necessary in order to ensure that holders of existing Common Shares and Junior Preferred Shares will not have rights more favourable than those of the holders of Series [●] Shares.

4.18 BOARD REPRESENTATION

A ONE-TIER SYSTEM VERSUS TWO-TIER SYSTEM

The term *board* does not hold uniform meaning. In certain jurisdictions (such as the US), a *one-tier board system* is the standard. In these jurisdictions, the term board refers to one comprised of executive as well as non-executive directors. In other jurisdictions, the concept of non-executive directors does not exist. In these jurisdictions, a two-tier board system applies and a distinction is made between a *management board* and a *supervisory board*, each constituting a separate corporate body within the company. Finally, there are jurisdictions where companies can opt for either a one-tier board system or a two-tier board system.

Regardless of the system followed with regard to the board, there is, in general, a clear distinction between the duties and responsibilities of the executive board members and those of the non-executive or supervisory board members. Since the separation of duties and responsibilities in a two-tier system is more evident than in the one-tier system, we will only discuss the two-tier board. Consequently, henceforth reference will be made only to the concepts *management board* and *supervisory board*.

B SUPERVISORY BOARD

The primary function of the supervisory board is to oversee the policy pursued by management and assess the general state of affairs in the company. The supervisory board advises the management board on specific issues, either on request or on its own initiative as required. The supervisory board normally has approval rights with respect to all important actions by the management board (see *section 20 – Consent Rights*, of this chapter). These functions of the supervisory board make it the perfect forum for venture capital investors to monitor the company and its management and to be involved in all decisions that are of fundamental importance to the company. Therefore, the investor will want to have the right to appoint or nominate one or more members of the supervisory board in almost all venture capital transactions.

Having a representative on the supervisory board will give the investor intimate knowledge of company affairs. It will in addition give the investor a tool to guide the company in the direction he deems best for the company. For the board to function well, not only the representative(s) of the investor, but also all the other members of the supervisory board should be knowledgeable in the company's field of operation. The composition and size of the supervisory board are very important to the success of a company and are often preconditions to financing. While the former should be the right mix of financial and commercial experts, as well as experts in the specific field(s) in which the company operates, the latter should be such as to enable it to function in an effective, flexible and transparent manner.

The duties and responsibilities of the supervisory board will differ in each jurisdiction, and investors should be aware of the legal position of the members of the supervisory board before nominating their representative to the board. Following are some of the basic rules that apply in most European jurisdictions.

The members of the supervisory board have collective powers and responsibilities. Consequently, in most European jurisdictions, they share responsibility for all decisions and acts undertaken by the supervisory board as well as those of each individual member of the supervisory board. The functions of the supervisory board do not include the exercise of executive functions, dispensing of specific instructions to the management board, determining the business policy of the corporation, or appointing or removing members of the management board. The supervisory board members may, however, adopt an independent stance vis-à-vis the management board and take measures to manage the company if the management board is unable to perform its duties (e.g. suspending members of the management board).

As a rule, the members of the supervisory board may be appointed and dismissed by the shareholders. Very often, direct appointment rights or special nomination rights are granted to holders of preferred shares. The shareholders' agreement should clearly state that they would undertake to vote in favour of persons so nominated in a shareholders' meeting.

The supervisory board is independent and not subordinate to the shareholders' meeting. In performing their duties, the members of the supervisory board are to be guided solely by the interests of the company and its business. It is important to note that irrespective of the course of appointment or nomination, each board member has fiduciary obligations towards the company. These obligations must always prevail over any obligations a board member may have to any other party. These fiduciary obligations may place board members appointed by an investor in an awkward position since they must always act in the best interest of the company, which may not always coincide with the best interest of the investor. The consequences of breaching fiduciary obligations can be serious and may result in personal liability for the debts of the company.

The supervisory board may form committees for specific areas of expertise depending on the specifics of the company and the number of members on the supervisory board. These committees serve to increase the efficiency of the supervisory board and the handling of complex issues. They are comprised of supervisory directors determined by the supervisory board, but may also be determined by the investors at the time of their investment. The committees are comprised of members who, as a whole, have the required knowledge, abilities, expertise and independence to properly perform their tasks within these committees. Commonly constituted committees are the *audit committee* and the *compensation committee*. The role of the audit committee is basically to assist the supervisory board in monitoring the integrity of the financial statements of the company, the independent auditor's qualifications, the performance of the company's internal audit function and the compliance by the company with legal and regulatory requirements. The primary objective of the compensation committee is to discharge the responsibilities of the supervisory board relating to compensation of the company's executive officers, such as salaries, stock option or other equity participation plans, the terms of employment agreements, severance arrangements, and any special or supplemental benefits. The purpose, role and responsibilities of the committees are often laid down in special committee charters.

A chairman may be elected on a supervisory board to co-ordinate the work within the supervisory board and its committees, and to chair the meetings. The chairman maintains regular contact with the management board and acts as the spokesperson of the supervisory board. Considering the amount of influence the chairman can exert, investors are generally keen on determining the chairman before they close their investment.

Supervisory board members and the members of its committees usually receive compensation for their efforts. The level of compensation is largely determined by the responsibilities and scope of tasks of the specific members of the supervisory board as well as the economic situation and performance of the company. Typically, the members of the supervisory board nominated (and employed) by the investors only receive reimbursement of expenses incurred by them in connection with the attendance of meetings of the supervisory board.

C **BOARD OBSERVATION RIGHTS**

It is sometimes impossible or inappropriate for an investor to have the right to nominate a member of the supervisory board, e.g. for reasons of size and composition of the board, or because of the amount invested by such an investor. Increased liability risk (and insurance premiums) and corporate governance codes (e.g. the Sarbanes-Oxley Act) can offer additional reasons for investors not to request or exercise nomination rights.

Investors that are not given a seat on the supervisory board may try to get a board observation right. A board observation right entitles the investor to have a representative (an *observer*) present at the board meetings and thus to closely monitor the company. In effect, this enables an investor to exert some influence at supervisory board meetings, without actually having a nominee on the supervisory board.

A board observer is not entitled to vote at the meetings of the supervisory board. Nevertheless, he will be entitled to attend the meetings of the company's supervisory board and will receive copies of all notices, written materials and other documentation provided to members of the supervisory board, provided that the company may withhold information or exclude the observer from meetings where required; for example to protect the attorney-client privilege or to protect highly confidential information. Since observers are usually not bound by the same fiduciary duties as the members of the supervisory board, they are required to enter into confidentiality agreements prior to exercising any observer rights.

D D&O INSURANCE AND INDEMNIFICATION

In cases where an investor has nominated a member to the supervisory board, he particularly wants to make sure that his nominee on the supervisory board is properly protected for liability asserted against him. Basically, there are two ways to protect the members of the supervisory board and members of the management board against such liability: firstly by executing an indemnification agreement and secondly by taking out directors' and officers' insurance (a *D&O insurance*).

An *indemnification agreement* is a contract between the company and a member of the supervisory or management board (a director) or other senior employees of the company (an officer) specifying that the company will compensate the director or officer for any costs incurred in defending the member against a lawsuit or similar complaint, or in settling such an action brought against him, provided the director or officer has not breached his fiduciary duties or committed fraud or been found grossly negligent.

A typical D&O insurance policy provides cover for the company and its directors and officers for claims arising from a wrongful act. However, D&O insurance policies generally contain a number of qualifications and limitations that narrow the scope of coverage. D&O insurance policies either indemnify the directors and officers, or reimburse the company for any monies it has paid out on behalf of the directors and officers.

An indemnification agreement can be a desirable addition to a D&O insurance policy, but should not be considered as a proper replacement for such insurance for several reasons. First, D&O insurance may insure against liabilities where indemnification is not allowed under the applicable corporate and insurance law. Second, due to various circumstances (e.g. change of managers, conduct of the director), the company may be permitted but unwilling to indemnify the individual. And third, the company may be unable to provide indemnification because it is insolvent. D&O insurance passes the risk and responsibility for indemnification on to a third party, the insurance company.

Board Representation:	The supervision of the policies by the Management Board and all other tasks and duties as assigned to it will be entrusted to the supervisory board (the "Supervisory Board"), which at Closing will consist of [___] members comprised of (i) [___] member(s) elected upon the nomination of the holders of a [qualified] majority of the Series [●] Shares (the "Series [●] Director"), (ii) [___] member(s) elected upon the nomination of the holders of the Preferred Shares, (iii) [___] elected upon the nomination of [[ ] (the "Founders')], and (iv) [___] person(s) who have specific expertise in the Company's field of business elected by a [qualified] majority of all shareholders and who are mutually acceptable [to the Founders and Investors][to the other directors]. [In addition, [name(s) Investor(s)][so long as it [they] hold(s) at least [___]% of the [Series [●] Shares] [outstanding shares] will have the right to designate one observer to the Supervisory Board, who will have the right to participate in discussions and to receive information, but will not be entitled to vote.] The Supervisory Board will meet at least [quarterly] with intermittent teleconferencing for at least the first [twelve (12)] months after Closing. The Company will pay the reasonable expenses incurred by members of the Supervisory Board in attending Supervisory Board meetings, including committee meetings, or otherwise representing the Company. Furthermore, [___] will receive an annual retainer of €[___] and a per-meeting fee of €[___].

[Following the Closing, the Supervisory Board will establish an audit committee and a compensation committee to be composed of the Series [●] Director and [___]. The compensation committee will be responsible for reviewing and approving all option grants, as well as compensation of officers of the Company and all non-officer employees whose annual salary exceeds €[___]

The Company will [maintain][take out] D&O insurance in the amount of at least €[five (5)] million per occurrence.

4.19 VOTING RIGHTS

Apart from sharing in the profits, it is a shareholder's basic right to vote in general shareholder meetings. This voting right enables each shareholder to participate in decisions concerning fundamental corporate issues.

In principle, each share entitles its holder to one vote. The assumption of equality of shares further entails that the holders of shares have equal voting rights in proportion to the nominal (par) value of the shares they hold. Nevertheless, in many European jurisdictions it is possible to have non-voting shares and even to have differential voting rights (e.g. double voting rights).

Term sheets may state that the holders of preferred shares will vote on an as-if converted basis; the preferred shares will then have a number of votes equal to the number of common shares issuable upon conversion of such preferred shares. Voting on an as-if converted basis is especially important if the conversion ratio has been, or may be, adjusted under the anti-dilution clause (see *section 14 – Anti-Dilution,* of this chapter). As mentioned above, in certain jurisdictions voting rights are connected to the actual nominal value of the shares involved. Such jurisdictions typically do not allow provisions in the articles of association stating that the voting rights attaching to certain types of shares shall be determined as if they were converted into common shares. In those cases, it will however be possible to agree contractually (typically in the shareholders' agreement) that this type of as-if converted system will apply. If the term sheet does not provide for any adjustment of the conversion ratio, there is no need to apply this as-if system, and preferred shares usually have the same voting rights as common shares.

Voting Rights: The holders of Series [●] Shares will vote together with the holders of Common Shares and not as a separate class except as specifically provided herein or as otherwise required by law. [Each Series [●] Share will have a number of votes equal to the number of Common Shares issuable upon conversion of such Series [●] Share.][Each Series [●] Share and Common Share will have one vote.]

4.20 CONSENT RIGHTS

The *consent rights* constitute one of the most important control instruments in venture capital transactions. Consent rights (also referred to as 'protective provisions') are effectively veto rights that investors have with respect to certain actions by the company, which they deem important.

From a legal perspective, actions taken by the company are based on resolutions made by its main corporate bodies – the general meeting of shareholders, the management board and the supervisory board. The power to make decisions concerning the operations of the company is vested in the management board, while all powers beyond the purview of the management or supervisory board, are vested in the general meeting of shareholders. The ultimate control in a regular private company is exercised by the shareholders' meeting, since it is entitled to dismiss and replace the management. In typical venture capital transactions, the investors hold minority positions and are thus unable to control the voting process in the general meeting of shareholders. Consent rights enable the investors to fill that gap.

Through their consent rights, investors are able to exert their influence both at shareholder level and at supervisory board level. By subjecting certain decisions of the general meeting of shareholders to the approval of the preferred shares (or of a specific class of preferred shares), the investors create a *blocking right* in their favour. Blocking rights can also be created by setting the required majority of votes for certain decisions of the general meeting of shareholders at such a high level, that *de facto* these decisions cannot be adopted without the investor's approval. Decisions subject to the approval of preferred shareholders typically include the issuance of securities, payment of dividends, entering into a merger and making of any amendments to the articles of association.

Investors exert their influence on management board decisions by subjecting them to prior approval of the supervisory board. The supervisory board normally has approval rights with respect to the following actions by the management board: changing of the nature of the company's business, approval of the annual budget and any non-budgeted expenses in excess of a predetermined amount, conducting of any litigation on behalf of the company, disposing of certain assets, and entering into any transactions with related parties.

Consent rights are also often referred to as *negative covenants*. A negative covenant is a legal promise *not* to take a certain action without the required prior consent. As opposed to negative covenants, every venture capital transaction also includes 'affirmative covenants'. Affirmative covenants are promises or obligations usually made by the company to take certain actions (instead of refraining from taking certain actions). For example, in the term sheet provided to *New Wave Energy* affirmative covenants are included in the following clauses: *Information Rights, Use of Proceeds, Employment Relationships, Key Man Insurance, Fees and Expenses,* and *Indemnities*.

Since consent rights limit the authority of the management board and the general meeting of shareholders, they are usually the subject of extensive negotiation by all concerned parties.

Consent Rights:	[Alternative 1: The Company's articles of association or any other constitutive corporate documents will be amended to contain restrictions making certain resolutions of the Management Board with a material effect on the Company's operations or management subject to the prior approval of the Supervisory Board and/or the holders of [Preferred Shares][Series [●] Shares], as the case may be. In addition, these documents will contain restrictions making certain resolutions of the general meeting of shareholders (e.g. resolutions regarding the structure and capitalisation of the Company) [subject to the prior approval of the holders of [Preferred Shares] [Series [●] Shares][subject to a qualified majority of votes].] [Alternative 2: The approval of a [qualified] majority of the Supervisory Board [including the Series [●] Director] and/or the holders of [Preferred Shares][Series [●] Shares] and/or a qualified majority of [two thirds/ three fourths] of the votes in the general meeting will be required for the following actions [unless provided for in the annual budget]: (i) engagement in any new line of business or jurisdiction where the Company is managed and controlled or any material modification of the business plan; (ii) approval of the annual budget and any non-budgeted expenses in excess of €[___]; (iii) implementation of an Employee Stock Option Plan and granting any rights thereunder; (iv) appointment of employees with a yearly salary in excess of €[___]; (v) disposal or acquisition of any securities in the capital of any other company or establishment of any new branch or subsidiary of the Company; (vi) exercise of voting rights in the shareholders' meeting of any subsidiary or affiliate, if any; (vii) conduct of any litigation on behalf of the Company; (viii) entering into a guarantee or indemnity or otherwise committing the Company (other than in the ordinary course of business);

(ix) provision of any loan or advance or any credit (other than in the ordinary course of business) to any person; (x) entering into any transactions with related parties; (xi) changing the accounting policies; (xii) entering into any agreements, contracts or arrangements that are not of an at arm's length nature; and (xiii) undertaking any such legal acts as will be determined and clearly defined by the Supervisory Board and notified to the Management Board in writing.

The approval of a [qualified] majority of the [Preferred Shares voting together as a class][Series [●] Shares] and/or a qualified majority of [two thirds/three fourths] of the votes in the general meeting will be required for the following actions: (i) issuance of any securities (including instruments convertible into securities and the issuance of subordinated debt); (ii) declaration and/or payment of any and all dividends by the Company; (iii) entering into any merger, consolidation, recapitalisation, change of control, or sale of all or substantially all of the assets of the Company; (iv) undertaking of any filing for bankruptcy, insolvency by or against the Company; (v) engagement in any transaction that constitutes a deemed dividend according to the relevant tax laws; and (vi) making of any amendments to the articles of association/charter/bylaws of the Company that adversely impact the [Preferred Shares][Series [●] Shares], including by way of merger, consolidation or otherwise.]

4.21 REGISTRATION RIGHTS

A INTRODUCTION

The *registration rights clause* deals with registration of the company's shares with the U.S. Securities and Exchange Commission (the *SEC*) so that they can be listed and traded on a U.S. stock exchange. In the U.S, shares may not be sold to the public unless they are registered (or an exemption from registration is available). Shares are registered by preparing a registration statement (which includes a prospectus) that must be filed with the SEC. The company must prepare the registration statement and vouch for the information contained within it. Consequently, it is impossible for investors to register shares without the co-operation of the company.

Since a sale of the company's shares to the public is an important exit opportunity for investors, they will at some point in time want to have the right to ensure that all necessary actions are undertaken to enable such a sale. A registration rights clause deals with this matter. It determines whether and under what circumstances investors have the right to demand registration. It also deals with the most important issues relating to registration. A registration rights clause is standard practice in U.S. term sheets. Outside the U.S. it is less common.

B DEMAND REGISTRATION VERSUS PIGGYBACK REGISTRATION

Basically, there are two types of registration rights: *demand registration rights* and *piggyback registration rights*. A demand registration right is the right of an investor to demand that his shares be registered. This gives an investor control over the timing of a registration and in effect means that the investor can force the company to go public. A piggyback registration right grants investors the right to include their shares in a registration initiated by another shareholder or the company.

Piggyback registration rights are less powerful than demand registration rights. They do not give investors the right to initiate a registration. Investors only have the right to *follow* in the process initiated and controlled by others and it is not in their power to force the company to go public. However, whereas the number of times that a demand registration right can be exercised is usually limited, piggyback registration rights clauses normally do not contain a limitation on the number of times the clause may be invoked.

C DEMAND REGISTRATION

The demand registration clause at the end of this chapter mentions two points at which registration may be demanded: (i) a certain period of time after the closing of the investment in the company, and (ii) a certain period of time after an IPO of the company's shares. If it is so agreed, investors can demand registration a certain period of time after closing (for example five years). In effect, this means the investors can force the company to go public once that period has elapsed. As stated above, an IPO is an important exit opportunity for investors and consequently investors prefer to have the right to force the company to go public after a certain passage of time. From the company's perspective, however, an IPO may not necessarily be very attractive. If, for example, the company believes it has not attained sufficient maturity to go public, a premature IPO may limit its possibilities to obtain funds in the future. Furthermore, publicly listed companies are subject to far more burdensome regulations than non-public companies. The company will therefore, normally, seek to go public only if it believes the circumstances are right. Because the support of the company and the board is important for a successful IPO, registration rights are rarely exercised. They can however provide the investors leverage in discussions on exit opportunities. During the negotiations between the company and the investors, a balance will have to be found between the interests of the investors and the interests of the company.

The second point at which registration may usually be demanded is several months after an IPO of the company's shares. Since this does not entail the right of the investors to enforce such a move, this issue does not usually give rise to any discussion between investors and the company. Most term sheets set the period after which registration may be demanded at six months after the IPO.

Registration is a costly and time-consuming affair. Consequently, it is usually agreed that the company will undertake all actions necessary for registration only if a certain specified percentage of the registrable shares are involved and the value of such shares exceeds a predetermined amount. The number of times that registration may be demanded is also usually limited. The frequency depends on several factors, such as the number of registrable shares and the liquidity of the market. If there are a large number of registrable shares, it may be wise to avoid *flooding* the market by registering all shares at the same time. In such cases, it may be appropriate to decide that registration may be demanded more times than in other cases. The same may apply in cases where a smaller number of shares are offered but the market is deemed relatively illiquid.

The final sentence in the demand registration clause below deals with situations where, for example, the number of shares offered pursuant to the exercise of a demand registration right is too large in the opinion of the underwriters. In such situations, the number of shares on offer may be limited (a *cutback*). The aforementioned sentence determines that the investors invoking the demand registration right will have priority in offering their shares over other shareholders who wish to register shares (such as investors invoking a piggyback registration right – see below).

D REGISTRATION ON FORM S-3

For a company that has already filed a registration statement with the SEC in the past and complies with all requirements relating to the registration of its securities, it seems only logical that a new registration of securities should be less burdensome and relatively less expensive than the initial registration. A registration on Form S-3 is intended for such cases.

A registration on Form S-3 is considered a short form registration and is much less burdensome and much cheaper than on Form S-1, which is used for an IPO or when a company is not eligible to use Form S-3. There are a number of requirements that a company must meet to use Form S-1. One of the mandatory qualification criteria for this type of registration is that the company in question must have offered its shares in an IPO that took place at least one year before the present S-3 registration.

E PIGGYBACK REGISTRATION

Most term sheets contain a *piggyback registration* clause. As stated earlier, such clauses grant investors the right to include their shares in a registration initiated by another shareholder or the company. In view of the fact that there is no limit to the number of shares that may be registered and the marginal costs of registering additional shares are relatively low, companies seldom object to granting piggyback registration rights.

Demand registration rights usually have priority over piggyback registration rights. Piggyback registration clauses therefore generally contain limitations on the right to sell shares in certain offerings. For example, if the underwriter determines that the market can only absorb a limited number of shares, the piggyback registration rights clause will usually provide for a limitation or even exclusion of the shares offered under this clause in favour of shares offered pursuant to the exercise of demand registration rights. Unlike *demand registration rights* clauses, *piggyback registration rights* clauses normally do not contain a limitation on the number of times the clause may be invoked.

F TRANSFER OF REGISTRATION RIGHTS

The factors governing transfer of registration rights vary from transaction to transaction. In certain transactions, it may be important for investors to have the option to freely transfer their rights to another company, for example a group company. In other transactions, transfer rights may be less important to investors and may be objectionable from the company's point of view. The company may also only accept transfer rights if the transferee obtains a certain minimum amount of shares.

G EXPENSES

Under normal circumstances, the company will pay the regular fees and expenses relating to the registration (filing fee, printing costs, accountant's fees, etc.) Whether or not the company will also pay (a part of) the fees and expenses of the investors' legal counsel, varies. Often, the company and the investors agree that the company will bear the reasonable fees and expenses of *one* legal counsel representing all registering shareholders. Often such fees and expenses are capped. Underwriting discounts and commissions and transfer taxes are usually borne by the investors.

H LOCK-UP

In most IPOs, underwriters require the largest shareholders and directors of the company to agree to a lock-up period of six months following the IPO. During that period they may not sell or transfer their shares. Registration rights clauses usually contain a provision stating that investors and members of the management board and supervisory board will agree to such a lock-up period. Very often the six months lock-up period is followed by an additional period of six months during which the investors are only allowed to sell their shares in block trades organized by the supporting investment banks. This prevents investors from dumping their shares and negatively influencing the share price.

I **OTHER REGISTRATION PROVISIONS**
The term sheet typically contains only the most important issues relating to registration rights. After the term sheet has been signed, these issues are usually dealt with more extensively in a separate agreement (usually referred to as the *Registration Rights Agreement*) to be entered into by the company or majority shareholders on the one hand, and the investors on the other.

J **EQUIVALENT RIGHTS**
The provisions of a registration rights clause deal with the U.S. concept of registration. By determining that an investor has the right to demand such registration, he is granted the opportunity to create an *exit* by offering his shares to the public. In (the many) cases where a public offering in the U.S. would, for whatever reasons, not be appropriate, investors will still wish to have the opportunity to create an exit by offering their shares to the public in another country. Sometimes an *equivalent rights* clause is included, to provide the investors such a possibility.

Registration Rights:	[Alternative 1: The holders of [Preferred Shares][Series [●] Shares] will have normal registration rights including demand registration rights, [unlimited] 'piggyback' registration rights, S-3 registration rights, transfer of registration rights, proportionate underwriter cutbacks, and other typical registration rights, all at the expense of the Company. The registration rights of all [Preferred Shares][Series [●] Shares] will be the same.]
	[Alternative 2: All Common Shares [issued or] to be issued upon conversion of the [Preferred Shares][Series [●] Shares] will be deemed "Registrable Securities".

Demand Registration: Upon the earliest of (i) [three-five] years after the Closing; or (ii) [six] months following an initial public offering ("IPO"), persons holding [30-50]% of the Registrable Securities may request [one][two] (consummated) registrations of their shares by the Company. The aggregate offering price for such registration may not be less than €[___] million. In the event of any cut-backs by the Company and/or its underwriters, shares to be registered by holders of Registrable Securities will have first priority for registration.

Registration on Form S-3: The holders of [10-30]% of the Registrable Securities will have the right to require the Company to register on Form S-3 (if available for use by the Company) Registrable Securities for an aggregate offering price of at least €[___] million. There will be no limit on the aggregate number of such Form S-3 registrations, provided that there are no more than [two] per year.

Piggyback Registration: The holders of Registrable Securities will be entitled to 'piggyback' registration rights on all registration statements of the Company, subject to the right, however, of the Company and its underwriters to reduce the number of shares proposed to be registered to a minimum of [30]% on a pro rata basis and to complete reduction on an IPO at the underwriter's discretion. In all events, the shares to be registered by holders of Registrable Securities will be reduced only after all other shareholders' shares are reduced.

Transfer of registration rights: The registration rights may be transferred to a transferee (other than to a competitor of the Company) who acquires at least €[___] of the shares held by a holder of [Preferred Shares] [Series [●] Shares]. [Transfer of registration rights to a group company of any Investor will be without restriction with regards to minimum shareholding.]

Expenses: The registration expenses (exclusive of share transfer taxes, underwriting discounts and commissions) will be borne by the Company. The Company will also pay the reasonable fees and expenses [not to exceed €___,] of one special counsel to represent all the participating shareholders.

Other registration provisions: Other provisions will be contained in the registration rights agreement with respect to registration rights as are reasonable, including cross-indemnification, the Company's ability to delay the filing of the demand registration for a period of not more than 120 days, the agreement by holders of [Preferred Shares][Series [●] Shares] if requested by the underwriter in a public offering not to sell any unregistered shares they hold for a period of up to 120 days following the effective date of the Registration Statement of such offering, the period of time during which the Registration Statement will be kept effective, underwriting arrangements and the like. [The registration rights will apply exclusively to Common Shares issued upon conversion of [Preferred Shares][Series [●] Shares] and the Company will have no obligation to register an offering of any other shares.]

If so requested by the managing underwriter, the holders of Preferred Shares will reach an agreement with regard to the IPO not to sell or transfer any Common Shares of the Company [(excluding shares acquired in or following the IPO)] for a period of up to 180 days following the IPO (provided all directors and officers of the Company and [1 – 5]% shareholders agree to the same lock-up).]

[In the event that the public offering as referred to in this 'Registration Rights' clause will or has taken place on a stock exchange outside the U.S, then the holders of Registrable Securities will be entitled to registration rights equivalent to the rights and obligations contained in this 'Registration Rights' clause (or as equivalent as possible given differences in applicable law).]

4.22 REPRESENTATIONS AND WARRANTIES

Representations and warranties are contractual guarantees afforded to a buyer by the seller regarding the nature and quality of the goods sold. In the context of venture capital financing, the representations and warranties are clauses usually contained in the investment agreement in which the company and/or the existing shareholders provide assurances to the investors regarding the status of the business and other matters, such as the company's capitalisation, key personnel, financial situation, liabilities, ownership, intellectual property, and compliance with all relevant laws.

Representations and warranties serve a variety of purposes. One important use for representations and warranties is that of a discovery tool; it is a method by which the investor forces the company to carefully consider the nature of its business, to gauge what it knows about its business and technology, and to reveal those facts on disclosure schedules that support the representations and warranties.

Warranties can be given *jointly* or *jointly and severally*. Only in the latter case is each guarantor liable for the whole amount.

If the term sheet is a binding document (which is usually not the case, see *section 44 – Non-Binding Character*, of this chapter), representations and warranties also provide the investor with the option to walk away if the due diligence process between the signing of the term sheet and the closing of the investment does not bear out the promises set out in the business plan. In such event the term sheet will contain a condition precedent in favour of the investor that allows the investor to terminate the investment process if it is determined that the results of the due diligence have not confirmed the assumptions of the investors regarding the status of the company (see *section 46 – Conditions Precedent*, of this chapter). If the term sheet is a non-binding document, it is generally not necessary to create a legal framework for breaking off negotiations.

Perhaps the most important aspect of representations and warranties, however, is their use as a risk allocation device for unknown factors. They determine who will bear the risk of liability (*who will give the guarantees?*) and to what extent (*what are the guarantees and what are the consequences of a breach?*). Warranties are provided for unknown liabilities. If at the time of signing, there are indications that a warranty has already been breached, then a specific indemnification clause should be included in the subscription agreement for the benefit of the investor. This is for two reasons: (i) thresholds and caps usually do not apply with respect to specific indemnities (which makes sense if the claim is known beforehand); and (ii) under some jurisdictions you lose the right to claim under a warranty if you knew beforehand there was a breach.

The term sheet will make clear which parties are required to provide the warranties. In some cases, the company is the only party providing the warranties. This is not always the preferred situation for investors. In some jurisdictions there is a risk that warranties granted by the company, in relation to an investment in the company, will be considered beyond the scope of the company's objects clause and will therefore be null and void. Furthermore, indemnification in case of breach of warranties granted by the company will be paid (at least partly) out of the investor's own pockets, since he will be one of the shareholders. Finally, if the breach of (one or more) warranties is so material that the shares of the company have become practically worthless (e.g. due to fraudulent acts or severe intellectual property issues) the company will not be able to pay any indemnification and the investor will have no recourse at all.

In other cases, all or some of the existing shareholders are required to provide warranties. Financial shareholders, such as the preferred shareholders from earlier rounds usually object to granting a full set of warranties. They will argue that (i) they are not involved on an operational level and therefore cannot be reasonably expected to grant warranties relating to the operation; and (ii) their investment funds are set up for a limited period of time and may well be liquidated before the expiration of the warranties. Sometimes they end up granting only a limited set of warranties, or a warranty insurance is used. In early-stage companies, where the founders have been closely involved in the business of the company, or even in a later-stage company where they hold a large percentage of the outstanding capital, investors may insist that the founders also make the representations and warranties personally. Such a personal warranty offers the investor some extra protection if the guarantor (i.e. the legal entity of the founder granting the warranties) appears to be an empty shell. Other forms of security for breach of warranties to ask from the guarantors are very limited. In a regular share purchase transaction, part of the purchase price is usually paid into an escrow account to give the purchaser some protection against breach of warranty; in venture capital transactions however, the full purchase price is transferred directly to the company (leaving aside any milestone payments). Theoretically, a right of pledge on the shares held by the guarantors could serve as security for the investor, but this is rarely seen in practice. Firstly, it is quite a hassle to effect and secondly, it does not provide any protection against breaches that are so material that they render the pledged shares worthless.

Further allocation of the risk of liability under the warranties will in general not be set forth in a term sheet, but in the investment agreement. This will become a subject of negotiation when the first draft of such agreement is distributed to the parties. Nevertheless, not all term sheets are alike, and some may include rather extensive representations and warranties clauses. In such cases, it is important to understand the most important aspects of representations and warranties at the term sheet stage.

As a rule, while negotiating the risk allocating factors in the representations and warranties, the investor will seek to implement an absolute warranty. The company on the other hand, will try to limit the warranty to known facts, or by adding qualifying phrases such as "to the best knowledge, information and belief" or "after due inquiry". Furthermore, the investors will try to use expanded definitions of the warranties in order to broaden their scope, while the company will try to narrow the definitions down as much as possible. Claims based on information that was fairly disclosed during the due diligence investigation are sometimes excluded from the scope of the warranties.

Using indemnification clauses, the investors seek to obtain the ultimate protection against a company's breach of a representation or non-fulfilment of a covenant, or against liabilities that arose prior to closing. The company, on the other hand, attempts to limit the investors' indemnification rights in several ways, e.g. by implementing *thresholds* or *baskets* requiring that one single claim and/or the aggregate claims must exceed a certain level before recovery will become available, and a *ceiling* or *cap*, a maximum aggregate amount for all claims for damages (usually the amount invested by each investor or a percentage thereof). Finally, the company will try to restrict the period during which the investors have the right to claim such damages as much as possible.

Representations and Warranties:	The investment agreement or a separate representation and warranties agreement will include standard representations and warranties granted by the [Company] [Founder] [Management Board] [and existing shareholders], [including, but not expressly limited to: (i) organisation and good standing; (ii) capitalisation structure; (iii) due authorisation; (iv) valid share issuance; (v) governmental consents; (vi) no company litigation; (vii) ownership or exclusive license of intellectual property rights; (viii) employees; (ix) pension plans; (x) assurances of full disclosure and accuracy of information provided; (xi) good title to all assets; (xii) tax; (xiii) accuracy of financial statements; (xiv) absence of adverse developments; and (xv) material contracts].

4.23 INFORMATION RIGHTS

In order to be able to monitor the company during the period of its investment, an investor will require certain specific financial and operational information of the company. If an investor is a minority shareholder and is neither represented on the supervisory board nor has a board observation right, he will only have limited access to the company's information, often too little to adequately monitor the company's business processes and progress.

The information rights required by investors may include the right to (i) consult with and advise the management of the company on significant business issues, and/or (ii) examine the books and records of the company and inspect its facilities and/or (iii) request specific information. Furthermore, the investors may want to receive certain pre-agreed monthly, quarterly and/or annual financial and operational information and, if an investor is not represented on the supervisory board, copies of all notices, minutes, consents and other material connected with such board meetings.

The obligation to provide access to any information of the company may be limited in order to preserve highly confidential proprietary information or to protect the attorney-client privilege. In order to avoid impractical and burdensome disclosure requirements on the part of the company, the group of shareholders who may have such information rights may also be limited. This can be done, for example, by limiting such access to shareholders holding a certain minimum number of (preferred) shares. For obvious reasons, shareholders that are competitors of the company will usually be excluded from the group of shareholders with extensive information rights.

Access to the company's information is normally terminated when a company is preparing for listing at a stock exchange (e.g. sixty days prior to the estimated filing date for an IPO) in order to comply with the applicable securities laws.

Information Rights:	[Any holder of Series [●] Shares][As long as the holders of [Preferred Shares][Series [●] Shares] [(provided that they are not a competitor of the Company)] continue to hold at least [___] [Preferred Shares][Series [●] Shares], they] will be granted access to Company facilities and personnel during normal business hours and with reasonable advance notification. The Company will deliver to such shareholder(s) (i) un-audited financial statements within 120 days after the end of the calendar year; (ii) quarterly [and monthly] financial statements within 20 days after such period, and other information as determined by the Supervisory Board; (iii) thirty days prior to the end of each fiscal year, a comprehensive operating budget forecasting the Company's revenues, expenses, and cash position on a month-to-month basis for the upcoming fiscal year; and (iv) promptly following the end of each quarter, an up-to-date capitalisation table, certified by the CFO. The foregoing provisions will terminate upon a Qualified Offering.

4.24 USE OF PROCEEDS

Most financing rounds result in the company receiving substantial amounts of money. It is of great importance to the investors that the company use these amounts in line with the agreed business plans and budget, and not for purposes such as the servicing of existing debt obligations (e.g. immediately after the closing). Investors generally have the ability to influence the company's spending using their consent right in the supervisory board and preferred shareholders' meeting. Nevertheless, very often investors want to have a specific guarantee (or *covenant*) from the company that it will use the proceeds from the investment round in accordance with the agreed plans and budget. Such a covenant is set out in a *Use of Proceeds* clause. These clauses typically define in general wording that the proceeds of the round are to be used as 'working capital', or more specifically, "for the expansion of the company's business, development of new products, marketing of its products, or achievement of initial revenue". If the use of proceeds is linked to milestones, the investors are able to monitor the company's spending after closing even better.

Use of Proceeds:	The Company will apply the net proceeds of the sale of the Series [●] Shares to the Investors exclusively to the development and operation of the Company in accordance with a business plan (including key milestones) and a 12-month budget to be [agreed upon by the Company and the Investors] [approved by the Investors] prior to Closing.

4.25 PRE-EMPTIVE RIGHTS

A *pre-emptive right* clause describes a shareholder's right to purchase his pro rata portion of any issuance of shares or other securities at the same price and on the same terms and conditions as applicable to other buyers of such securities. The pre-emptive right enables the existing shareholders to maintain their fractional ownership of the company.

In most European countries, a pre-emptive right is automatically provided to the shareholders by law. It may be excluded in the articles of association or limited to holders of the same class of shares to be issued (a general exclusion) or by resolution of the general meeting of shareholders if the articles so permit (a specific exclusion). Instead of excluding the pre-emptive right, shareholders may also agree in advance (e.g. in the shareholders' agreement) that they will waive their pre-emptive right under certain circumstances. In the US on the other hand, a pre-emptive right is not automatically provided to the shareholders by law. Instead, the pre-emptive rights are only considered valid if explicitly agreed between the company and its shareholders (i.e. in a shareholders' agreement or an investors' rights agreement). It is a highly negotiated right and is usually provided only to a few select (major) investors, to avoid undue complication of subsequent financing rounds as also to ensure that a certain number of securities offered in subsequent rounds will be available for purchase by new investors.

Usually, the company and its shareholders agree to exclude certain issuances of securities from the pre-emptive right. These exclusions, or *carve-outs*, are *inter alia* to allow the company to comply with the employee stock option plan or to facilitate proper execution of a merger or IPO. These and other such carve-outs are set out in more detail in the last paragraph of the *Pre-Emptive Right* clause below and are similarly applicable to the anti-dilution protection (see *section 14 – Anti-Dilution,* of this chapter).

A pre-emptive right is also referred to as a *right of first offer*, *pre-emption right*, *subscription privilege*, *right of first refusal at issuance* or *subscription right*.

Keep in mind that, even if a specific exclusion of pre-emptive rights is allowed according to the articles of association, some jurisdictions apply principles of general corporate law – such as equal rights for all shareholders – which call for additional justification for this differential treatment. If flexibility is required in respect of pre-emptive rights, make sure the shareholders agreement and articles provide an adequate basis for such flexibility.

Pre-emptive Rights:	Without prejudice to the 'Anti-Dilution' clause, if the Company proposes to offer equity securities, or securities convertible into or exchangeable for shares, the holders of [Preferred Shares][Series [●] Shares] will be entitled to purchase (...)

[Alternative 1: (...) on a pro rata basis all or any portion of such securities. Any securities not subscribed for by a holder of [Preferred Shares][Series [●] Shares] may be reallocated among the other holders of [Preferred Shares][Series [●] Shares]. If holders of [Preferred Shares][Series [●] Shares] do not purchase all of such securities, the portion that is not purchased may be offered to the other shareholders on terms not less favourable to the Company for a period of [60] days.]

[Alternative 2: (...) such securities in an amount sufficient to allow the holders of [Preferred Shares][Series [●] Shares] to retain their fully diluted ownership of the Company.]

[The pre-emptive right will not apply in the event of issuances of (i) Common Shares issued or issuable to employees, consultants or directors of the Company directly or pursuant to the ESOP (as set out in the 'Employee Pool' clause) that have been approved by the Supervisory Board; (ii) Common Shares issued or issuable upon conversion of the Preferred Shares; (iii) Common Shares issued or issuable in connection with a merger, acquisition, combination, consolidation or other reorganisation involving the Company approved by the Supervisory Board of the Company; (iv) Common Shares issued or issuable in connection with (a) any borrowings from a commercial lending institution, (b) the lease of equipment or property by the Company, or (c) strategic partnerships and/or licensing relationships, so long as such transactions are approved by the Supervisory Board; and (v) Common Shares issued or issuable (a) in a public offering before or in connection with which all outstanding Preferred Shares will be converted to Common Shares or (b) upon exercise of warrants or rights granted to underwriters in connection with such a public offering.]

4.26 RIGHTS OF FIRST REFUSAL

A *right of first refusal* is a right of a shareholder to meet the terms of a third party's offer if another shareholder intends to sell his shares to such third party. The purpose of the right of first refusal is to keep the company's shares in friendly hands, and to allow the existing shareholders to benefit from a sale of company shares if they are offered at an attractive price

Negotiations regarding the right of first refusal clause usually focus on two important elements of the clause: the shareholders holding the right of first refusal, and the shareholders granting it. The (common) shares held by the founders and key employees are usually fully subject to a right of first refusal or even a lock-up period, during which they are not allowed to be sold at all without the investors' approval (see *section 32 – Founders' Shares*, of this chapter). Investors in their capacity as holders of preferred shares typically insist on having a right of first refusal, but may resist granting it because of its negative effect on the marketability of the shares. Future buyers may be reluctant to make an offer for shares that are subject to a right of first refusal unless they receive a discount upon eventual purchase or are promised some kind of compensation if and when the right is exercised.

The right of first refusal should be read in conjunction with the co-sale right (see *section 27 – Co-Sale Right*, of this chapter) and drag-along right (see *section 28 – Drag-Along Right*, of this chapter), since in most cases a third party will only be interested in buying all of the company's shares and not only a portion thereof.

Sometimes a right of first refusal clause also provides for a forfeiture of such right if not all shares so offered are subscribed for. The selling shareholder is then free to sell all, but usually not less than all, of these shares to the proposed buyer.

The price payable for the shares offered under the right of first refusal is generally the price at which the potential buyer is prepared to purchase the shares. Sometimes however, this price is determined by taking the lower of (i) the price offered by the potential buyer and (ii) the market value, as determined by an independent expert.

Exceptions to the right of first refusal generally apply to transfers approved by a (qualified) majority of the general meeting of shareholders or transfers by an investor to a member of his group. Rights of first refusal normally terminate upon a public offering or sale of the company.

A right of first refusal is usually set out in a shareholders' agreement or in a separate *right of first refusal and co-sale agreement*, but it may also be included in the articles of association of the company. In certain European jurisdictions specific legal requirements may apply. A right of first refusal is also referred to as a *pre-emptive right*. In this book however, the term *pre-emptive right* will solely be used in the context of a right to pre-empt in case of *new share issues* by the company.

Rights of First Refusal:	[Holders of [Preferred Shares][Series [●] Shares]][The Company first and holders of [Preferred Shares][Series [●] Shares] second (or vice versa)] have a right of first refusal with respect to any [share(s) in the Company][Common Share(s)][and securities convertible into or exchangeable for shares] proposed to be sold by [a shareholder][Founder][and employees holding more than [1]% of the outstanding Common Shares (assuming conversion of the Preferred Shares)], at the same price and on the same terms as offered, with a right of over-subscription for holders of [Preferred Shares][Series [●] Shares] of [share(s) in the Company][Common Share(s)][and securities convertible into or exchangeable for shares] un-subscribed by the other holders of [Preferred Shares][Series [●] Shares].
	The right of first refusal will not apply in the event of (i) a transfer of shares approved by a majority of [75]% of the voting rights; or (ii) a transfer by a holder of Preferred Shares to an affiliate.

Such right of first refusal will terminate upon the earlier of (i) ten years from the Closing Date; (ii) a Qualified Offering; (iii) a sale or merger of the Company; [(iv) with respect to any employee, when such employee no longer owns any Common Shares]; [(v) with respect to any holder of [Preferred Shares][Series [●] Shares], when such holder of [Preferred Shares][Series [●] Shares] no longer owns at least [___] [Preferred Shares][Series [●] Shares]].

4.27 CO-SALE RIGHT

A *co-sale right* or *tag-along right* is a shareholder's contractual right to include his shares in any sale of shares by another shareholder under the same terms and conditions.

If the shareholders have agreed to a right of first refusal (which is typically the case) the co-sale right should be read in conjunction with the right of first refusal, since it is only exercisable to the extent that the right of first refusal is not (or partly) exercised. Shareholders, who may be free to transfer their shares under the right of first refusal clause, may therefore nevertheless be required to allow the investors to include (a portion of) their shares in the sale.

The co-sale right provides each shareholder with the right to benefit from a third-party sale. Sometimes only the investors are entitled to a co-sale right.

If shareholders exercise their co-sale right, they will participate in a sale arranged by another shareholder at the same price and under the same terms and conditions. The level of such participation will be set forth in the final legal documentation, but is usually calculated on a pro rata basis.

Example: If a selling founder who owns 100 shares in the company has agreed to sell 50 shares to a third party, an investor holding 400 shares will be allowed to co-sell 40 shares (being 400/500*50) of the total number of 50 shares to be sold (assuming no other investors exercise their co-sale right), whereas the selling founder will only be allowed to sell ten shares. Investors may require the right to co-sell more than their pro rata share (up to 100%)

in exceptional circumstances, for example in the event that the purchaser is a competitor or a customer of the company or if such purchaser would acquire a controlling stake in the company.

The co-sale rights clause is a contractual right granted to (certain) shareholders and is usually set out in the shareholders' agreement or in a separate *right of first refusal and co-sale agreement*. In order to allow free trade in the company's listed shares, the co-sale right should terminate upon the company's initial public offering (IPO).

Co-Sale Right: Before any shareholder may sell shares in the Company, after having observed the terms and procedures of the 'Right of first Refusal' clause, he will give [the other Shareholder] [the holder of [Preferred Shares][Series [●] Shares] an opportunity to participate in such sale on a pro rata basis.

4.28 DRAG-ALONG RIGHT

A *drag-along right* is a right that enables the investors to force a sale of the company. Effectively, it is an agreement between all shareholders (therefore generally found in the shareholders' agreement) to sell their shares, if a (qualified) majority of the preferred shareholders (and/or other shareholders) are in favour of such a sale, and to take all other actions necessary and desirable in connection with such a sale in the future. A merger of the company (resulting in a change of control) or a sale of the company's assets is usually included in the scope of a drag-along right.

The drag-along right enables the investors to sell the company regardless of the fact that they may only hold a minority stake in the company and notwithstanding that the other shareholders (e.g. founding shareholders, or shareholders having no deemed liquidation rights) and management board and supervisory board may not be supportive of the deal. This ability provides the investors with control over the execution and timing of the sale of the company, which has a positive effect on the sales price and eases the process of pre-sale marketing and negotiations.

The drag-along clause comes in many flavours. One element in the drag-along clause that needs specific attention is the definition of *sale of the company*. The definition of *sale of the company* in the clause may be drafted *broadly*, including all transactions listed in the 'liquidation preference' clause (so-called *(deemed) liquidation events*), or *restrictedly*, reflecting only the sale of shares in the company or, more restrictedly, the sale of all shares of the company. In all cases, the drag-along clause in the final documentation should make clear that the proceeds from such a transaction are to be distributed in accordance with the liquidation preference clause. To prevent an investor from misusing his drag-along right to squeeze out one or more shareholders, it is usually required that the drag-along right can only be triggered in case of a *third party* offer.

In the term sheet or final documentation, it is usually set out to what extent the shareholders who are forced to sell their shares, are required to provide representations and warranties to the buyer. This ranges from the most basic and essential representations and warranties only (typically those regarding the legal title of their shares and their (unrestricted) transferability) to the same warranties that the investor triggering the drag-along right provides himself.

Another important element is the class (or classes) of shareholders and the majorities required to trigger the drag-along right. Investors will understandably want to keep this group as small as possible, while the other parties involved may want to include an approval right of the general meeting of shareholders. Other issues of negotiation may concern the inclusion of limitations in time (the drag-along right becomes valid only after a certain period of time) and of a minimum amount of required proceeds (the drag along can be triggered only if a certain minimum amount of anticipated proceeds will result from the sale). These restrictions are aimed at preventing the investors from selling the company soon after closing at a good return (for them), whereas the other shareholders may not necessarily receive a similarly good return (since the liquidation preference applies). Sometimes a matching right is negotiated to prevent the investor from effectuating a sale of the company below market price. Investors are generally reluctant to accept a matching right for the other shareholders, or only for very short periods of time, since they are afraid that a third-party bidder may walk away if the matching process takes too much time.

The drag-along right typically terminates if the company undertakes a public offering.

Drag-Along Right:	[Alternative 1: The holders of a [qualified] majority of the [Preferred Shares][Series [●] Shares] may require a sale of the entire issued share capital of the Company.] [Alternative 2: In the event, [that a third party makes an offer to acquire all of the outstanding shares of the Company][of a Deemed Liquidation Event], that is accepted by the holders of a [qualified] majority of the [Preferred Shares][Series [●] Shares], the other shareholders will be obliged to [vote in favour of such Deemed Liquidation Event and to take all actions necessary in connection therewith][offer their shares to said third party under the same terms and conditions specified in such offer] and accordingly (to the extent necessary) waive their rights of first refusal etc.] [If the holders of the [Preferred Shares][Series [●] Shares] wish to exercise the drag-along right as set out in the previous paragraph within [___] years after the Closing, the additional approval of the holders of a [qualified] majority of the outstanding Common Shares (assuming conversion of the Preferred Shares), will be required.]

4.29 MANAGEMENT BOARD

The *management board* is responsible for the day-to-day management of the company and for its representation vis-à-vis third parties.

The management board may consist of one or more members (*managing director(s)*). If the management board has more than one member, each member will have different responsibilities. As in US corporations, many European venture-backed companies use titles reflecting the responsibilities of each management board member, such as Chief Executive Officer (CEO) and Chief Financial Officer (CFO) and, in the case of technology companies, Chief Technology Officer (CTO). Several variations are possible in the composition and size of the management boards, depending on the development stage of the company. A start-up company may start out with only one member (the founder), while more mature companies will have the resources and the workload to set a full team to work.

Despite the fact that a division of tasks amongst the members of the management board is possible, it is important to note that in certain jurisdictions the management board is collectively responsible for all members of such board.

The members of the management board are appointed and may also be dismissed by the shareholders. In most European jurisdictions, a member of the management board may also be suspended by the shareholders, and/or if the company has a supervisory board in place, by the supervisory board.

From a strictly legal point of view, the management board is not subordinate to the shareholders' meeting or the supervisory board and is independent in the performance of its duties. In venture capital transactions, the boundaries of this independence are narrowed down considerably by protective provisions such as consent rights. Under such provisions, the approval of the majority of the preferred shareholders is required for important management (and shareholders) decisions, and the consent of the supervisory board is required for other important decisions. The consent matters are set out in more detail in *section 20 – Consent Rights*, of this chapter.

Management Board:	The management of the Company will be entrusted to the management board (the "Management Board") consisting at Closing of [___] as chief executive officer and [___] as chief [ ] officer. Any new Management Board members or senior company officers will not receive an offer of employment without the approval of the Supervisory Board [including the Series [●] Director]. [The Company will, on a best-efforts basis, hire a chief [___] officer within the [six (6)] month period following the Closing.]

4.30 EMPLOYEE POOL

A EMPLOYEE STOCK OPTIONS

An *employee stock option* is a right granted to an employee of a company to buy a common share in the company's capital at a pre-set price (*exercise price*) within a specified period of time (*exercise period*). If the value of the company increases during the exercise period of an option, the holder of such an option can benefit from such option by buying the underlying share at the exercise price, which is less than the actual value of said share. In theory, the holder of the option has made a profit. He will, however, not be able to cash this profit until the moment he actually sells such a share. This will generally only be possible upon a sale of the company, or upon a listing of the company on a stock exchange. As the basic principles of a venture-backed company include the aim to increase value and to pursue liquidity for its investors through a sale or IPO of the company, the granting of employee options is considered one of the most effective incentive tools available to the company.

The shares reserved for the purpose of issuance upon the exercise of outstanding options are collected in an *employee pool* or *option pool*. The terms and conditions under which the employee options can be granted, exercised and transferred are usually set out in an arrangement called *employee stock option plan* or ESOP. The number of shares reserved in the option pool is typically ten to fifteen percent of the fully diluted share capital of the company. As detailed in *section 7 – Share Price and Valuation*, of this chapter, investors will consider the full option pool, *including* the non-granted options, as outstanding stock for the purpose of calculating the price per share.

If at a new financing round it is decided to increase the option pool, new investors may try to negotiate to have the increase *pre-money* so the dilution from the option pool allocation comes from the shares of the existing investors and founders only.

The supervisory board, sometimes represented by its special *compensation committee*, is the corporate body to which the power to decide on the terms of the ESOP and to grant options under the ESOP is normally delegated.

Unfortunately for employees and investors, the tax authorities in many European countries have curbed the advantages of stock options by implementing stringent rules. Typical taxable events are the granting, the vesting and the exercising of the options. These in turn can reduce the ESOP's effectiveness as an incentive tool.

B EMPLOYEE STOCK OWNERSHIP

Instead of granting employees options to buy shares in the future, they can also be offered the opportunity to buy shares at once. In some jurisdictions, the subsequent increase in value of these shares is not taxed at all, provided that the shares are acquired by the employee at an arm's length price. To finance the share purchase, the company may grant a loan to the employee.

In some cases, companies do not offer common shares to employees, but non-voting shares, *depository receipts* of shares or shares carrying other restrictions instead. The employees who buy shares or equivalents of shares usually are bound by an incentive plan called Employee Stock Ownership Plan, Restricted Stock Ownership Plan or Share Purchase Plan.

Such an incentive plan is typically subject to a repurchase clause and a vesting clause (see *section 31 – Vesting Scheme*, of this chapter). The purpose of this combination of a repurchase clause and a vesting clause is to ensure that the company can repurchase the non-vested stock from the employee upon termination of the employment agreement at the price originally paid by the employee (or the lower market value).

C OTHER INCENTIVE SCHEMES

In addition to stock option and stock ownership plans, other employee incentive schemes exist. Examples of such schemes are stock appreciation rights and dynamic equity splits.

Stock appreciation rights or SARs are awards that enable employees to profit from an increase in value of the company. SARs provide the employee with a bonus payment based on the increase in the value of a stated number of shares over a specific period of time. These proceeds will usually be paid in cash, but can also be paid in shares, or in a combination of cash and shares, depending on the rules of the incentive plan. Pay-outs under SARs are usually taxed as ordinary income. Stock appreciation rights are also known as phantom stock.

Recently, other incentive schemes have been developed to motivate and retain employees, in particular for early-stage start-ups. One of them is the *dynamic equity split*. With a dynamic equity split the idea is that everyone involved in the early stage of a start-up (which includes founders, employees, advisors, etc.) is rewarded for his contribution during this stage of the start-up. Contribution can be in hours of work, but also by providing equity or introducing a first customer. Based on an agreed calculation method, rewards are converted into real equity at a later time, for example when a Series A investment round takes place.

> **Employee Pool:** Upon the Closing, the Company will reserve up to [[number of shares] Common Shares][[___]% of the post-money outstanding shares] for issuance to employees, directors and consultants (the "Reserved Employee Shares") [including the Common Shares presently reserved for issuance upon the exercise of outstanding options]. The Reserved Employee Shares will be issued from time to time under [such arrangements, contracts or plans][an employee share option plan (the "ESOP")] as [recommended by the Management Board and] approved by the Supervisory Board.

4.31 VESTING SCHEME

A INTRODUCTION

Most ESOPs and stock ownership plans are subject to *vesting*. The concept of vesting refers to a pre-condition on the right to dispose over the stock (options). The purpose of a vesting scheme is to create a longer-term incentive for the employees. If an employee leaves the company shortly after having been granted stock (options), he should be able to benefit from such stock (options) only to a limited extent or not at all. In addition, a vesting mechanism is a valuable instrument to control dilution and to allow the company to conserve its equity.

Under a vesting scheme, the beneficiary of an ESOP or stock ownership plan can dispose over more stock (options) as time passes. Vesting periods are often fixed at three to five years. Vesting usually occurs on a monthly or quarterly basis. Shares and options under an ESOP may be subject to *cliff vesting*. This means that an employee has to remain with the company for a certain period, usually six to twelve months, before any stock (option) is to be considered vested. The vesting schedule obviously depends on the specifics of each transaction. In certain cases, a shorter period will be appropriate; in others a longer one will be logical. Sometimes a linear vesting system may be put in force (i.e. the number of shares vesting per time period is fixed), while, in other cases, a non-linear system (i.e. the number of shares vesting per time period varies) would be more appropriate. In case of a liquidity event (an exit) it is usually determined that all non-vested shares will vest at once, which is referred to as *accelerated vesting*.

Example: *Let us assume that an employee is granted 1,000 stock options. Assume also that the options are subject to a 4-year vesting scheme at the rate of 1/48th of the total number of options each month. Consequently, after one year the employee can freely dispose over 250 options.*

The remaining 750 options have not yet vested and consequently cannot be freely disposed over by the employee. After 2.5 years, the employee can freely dispose over 625 options (etc.). If the employee leaves the company before all his options have vested, he forfeits the options that have not yet vested at that time. If a twelve month cliff vesting scheme applied, then the employee would forfeit all of his 1,000 options if he left the company within one year after he has received the options, despite the monthly vesting. If the company is being sold while an employee is employed by the company, such employee can exercise all of his options, whether they have been vested or not.

Under a vesting scheme relating to a stock ownership plan, an employee who leaves the company is allowed to keep only those shares that vested during his tenure. The shares that have not vested will be repurchased by the company – assuming the applicable law allows this. If such is not the case, the shares may be repurchased by the other shareholders on a pro rata basis. Such retroactive vesting is also referred to as a *reverse vesting scheme*. By agreeing to a vesting period that reflects the expected growth speed of the company, a fair system can be created that will allow employees who leave earlier to benefit only from the growth that can (in part) be attributed to their efforts.

Apart from addressing the *free ride* issue, a vesting system can serve to comfort an investor with regard to the commitment of the employees. It acts as a *golden handcuff* system; the employees have a clear incentive to stay with the company for a longer period.

B GOOD LEAVER/BAD LEAVER

The vesting system can be further refined by distinguishing between a *good leaver* and a *bad leaver*. If the employee leaving the company is a *good leaver*, he could for example be entitled to keep his vested shares, while his non-vested shares will be repurchased at the price originally paid. If he is a *bad leaver*, it could be determined the vested and non-vested shares will be repurchased at the nominal value of the shares or the price originally paid (assuming that the price originally paid is lower than the fair market value). Bad leaver situations will be defined in the shareholders' agreement and usually include gross misconduct and leaving the company to join a competitor. All other circumstances are then considered good leaver situations. Sometimes there is also a third category, the neutral leaver, which will include death and retirement and restrict the good leaver to dismissal without cause.

Vesting Scheme:	All Reserved Employee Shares will be subject to vesting as follows: [25]% to vest at the end of the first year following their issuance, with the remaining [75]% to vest monthly over the next [three] years. Good leaver/bad leaver provisions will apply.

4.32 FOUNDERS' SHARES

A substantial percentage of the shares in the company is usually owned by one or more founders. If all goes as planned, all founders will stay with the company and contribute to its success. However, all does not always go as planned. It is therefore sensible to think about contingencies such as that of one or more founders holding shares in the company leaving the company earlier than planned. Can they keep their shares? Is it fair to let them *free ride* on the efforts of those who continue to build the company? Do they have to offer their shares and if so for what price? For the reasons set out in the *Vesting Scheme* clause (see *section 31 – Vesting Scheme*, of this chapter), investors may wish to subject all outstanding common shares held by the founders to a *reverse vesting scheme* to ensure continued commitment of the founders towards the progress of the company. Many of the terms that apply to the vesting of founders' shares are identical to those that apply to the vesting of employee shares (see *section 31 – Vesting Scheme*, of this chapter).

For founders, good leaver and bad leaver provisions can have a huge impact. They should carefully consider who has the power to dismiss them as managing directors of the company. If it is the investor, they should be aware that a dismissal could trigger the obligation to offer their shares under the applicable leaver provisions. Moreover, they should carefully consider the definition of a bad leaver, as this regularly leads to heated discussions.

If a founder has to offer his shares under an applicable good leaver provision, two complications often arise: (i) it can be very hard to determine what the market value is, in particular in case of an early-stage start-up, and (ii) the company will not always have the cash to buy out a founder. For those two reasons, the investors and other remaining shareholders sometimes negotiate the right to force a leaving founder to convert his shares into non-voting shares. By doing so, the leaving founder will lose all of his voting powers, while keeping his economic interest.

Founders' Shares:	Upon the Closing, [number of shares] of the Company's issued and outstanding Common Shares will be held by the Founders (the **"Founders' Shares"**). The Founders' Shares will be subject to a similar vesting scheme as set forth in the 'Vesting Scheme' clause, provided that the vesting period will begin as of the Closing. [In addition, in the event that the Company milestones are not satisfied, the Company will have the right upon termination of employment of a Founder with or without cause, to repurchase his vested Founders' Shares in the Company at fair market value (as determined by the Supervisory Board).]

4.33 LOCK-UP

Founders and key employees of venture-backed companies often own a significant quantity of common shares of the company, which they have received in exchange for their contribution of unique skills or intellectual property to the company. Before making an investment in a company, investors want to ensure that the key employees (including the founders) will continue their employment with the company and are committed to its future success. In order to achieve that goal, investors may insist on making the shares held by the founders and key employees subject to reverse vesting as set out in the *Founders Shares* clause. In addition, investors may insist that the founders' (and key employees') shares are subjected to a lock-up agreement, preventing them from selling their vested shares without the approval of the investors.

A lock-up of founders' shares as mentioned in this clause however, should not be confused with a lock-up agreement in connection with an anticipated listing at a stock exchange. The latter is typically executed as a requirement from the underwriters and is aimed at preventing the company's shareholders from selling their shares during a certain period following the listing at the stock exchange.

Lock-Up:	At no time prior to [date] will any Founder or key employee, if any, dispose of any shares in the Company in any manner, except with the written consent of [two-thirds] of the holders of Series [●] Shares. This lock-up will in any case lapse at the consummation of a Qualified IPO, trade sale or other liquidity event.

4.34 EMPLOYMENT RELATIONSHIPS

The terms and conditions of the *employment relationship* between an employer and an employee are usually set out in an employment agreement. The existence of proper employment agreements between the company and key employees is of great importance to most investors. It provides security with regard to their concerns regarding the company's continued access to the services, skills, and knowledge of its key employees.

Investors usually want to have a clear understanding of the terms of the employment agreements of the key employees, such as their duties and responsibilities, their compensation and other benefits (e.g. options and bonuses) during the employment term and upon termination, and the covenants provided by them, such as a non-compete, non-disclosure and assignment of inventions covenant, prior to a closing.

Employment Relationships: The Company has or will have prior to the Closing employment Closing employment agreements in a form reasonably acceptable to the Investors with [the following persons: [names]][each Founder and key employee].

4.35 NON-COMPETITION/NON-SOLICITATION

In particular in early-stage venture capital transactions, investors base their investment decision on the continuing involvement of the founders, who have specific knowledge of the company's business and technology. The purpose of a non-competition (or *non-compete*) agreement is to deter the founders from leaving the company to work for, or as, a competitor, as this would probably jeopardise the company's future success. A standard clause in non-compete agreements is the *non-solicitation* clause, which prohibits a founder who leaves the company from approaching its customers and employees with the intention of recruiting them for his new venture.

Non-compete agreements limit a person's ability to engage in a designated profession, trade or business. Therefore, they will be enforced by law only if the provisions are carefully limited and are drafted in compliance with the particular requirements of non-compete laws of the applicable jurisdiction. The three most important elements of non-compete agreements are the *business* in which the founder is precluded from competing, the *geographic scope* of the non-compete, and the *duration* thereof (non-competes generally have a one or two year duration). Each of these elements should be proportionate to the legitimate business interest of the company. A non-compete/non-solicitation covenant is usually part of the shareholders' agreement.

As mentioned in the previous paragraph, it is crucial for the investor that key employees are bound by robust non-competition/non-solicitation provisions. In certain jurisdictions, non-compete restrictions in employment agreements are valid only if the employee is allowed an additional consideration in exchange for signing or executing such agreement. The company should therefore enter into non-compete agreements only if this is strictly necessary to protect its interests. In addition to the negative incentive created by a non-compete/non-solicitation clause, positive incentives such as share vesting agreements and ESOPs should be considered as an instrument to keep key employees with the company.

Negotiation tips:
- If the founder holds his shares through one or more other companies (i.e. the founder indirectly holds his founder's shares), it makes sense for the founder to also be bound by the non-competition agreement in his capacity as a private person. Otherwise, the founder-shareholder could easily evade the non-compete restriction by incorporating a new legal entity.
- A longer duration than is allowed under the applicable law will usually make the non-compete covenant null and void in its entirety. So make sure the clause is enforceable under applicable law.
- Make sure the shareholders agreement provides the (preferred) shareholders, and not just the company, with the right to initiate legal action against the key individuals in case of a breach of any non-competition covenant.

Non-Competition/Non-Solicitation:	Prior to Closing, each Founder and key employee will enter Non-Solicitation: into a [one] year non-competition and non-solicitation agreement in a form reasonably acceptable to the Investors.

4.36 NON-DISCLOSURE AGREEMENT

A non-disclosure agreement aims to protect the company against improper disclosure or use of sensitive company information and materials that are not known to the general public. In companies active in the life sciences areas for example, non-disclosure agreements are used to preserve un-filed patent rights, trade secrets, business plans, and other confidential and proprietary information.

Non-disclosure agreements between employers and their employees are typically included as a specific covenant by the employee in the employment agreements. For employees or consultants with specific knowledge of the company's proprietary information or access thereto, more extensive agreements may be appropriate.

In general, a non-disclosure agreement specifies the type of information deemed confidential. Such information may include unpublished patent applications, know how, financial information, business strategies, etc. A non-disclosure agreement typically sets out details of information excluded from the non-disclosure agreement. Common exceptions are with regard to information that (i) the recipient can demonstrate he was in possession of prior to having received such information from the discloser; (ii) becomes public through no initiation of the recipient; (iii) becomes known to the recipient through a third party that has a lawful right to disclose such information; (iv) was public knowledge before the disclosure of such information to the recipient; and (v) was independently created by the recipient. The non-disclosure agreement also typically clarifies that all tangible embodiments of the information (e.g, models, data, and drawings) and all copies thereof should be returned immediately upon request of the company and in no event later than the end of the (employment) agreement term. The term clause of the non-disclosure agreement stipulates the term (in years) during which the information should be kept confidential, and the term (in years) during which the agreement is binding.

To enforce a non-disclosure agreement, the enforcing party should be able to demonstrate the existence of confidential information within the definition of proprietary information and the unauthorised use thereof. Sometimes the non-disclosure agreement includes a penalty clause, which makes it easier for the enforcing party to prove damages that result from any unauthorised use of confidential information.

A *non-disclosure agreement* is often referred to as an NDA or a *confidentiality agreement* or a CDA.

Non-Disclosure Agreement:	Prior to Closing, each current and former Founder, and each officer, employee and consultant with access to the Company's confidential information/trade secrets will enter into a non-disclosure agreement in a form reasonably acceptable to the Investors.

4.37 ASSIGNMENT INVENTIONS

Intellectual property is the most valuable asset of many high tech and life sciences companies. It is also very important for emerging companies in other industries. Creating new intellectual property can be one of the most important value drivers of such companies. To ensure that the company is the owner of the proprietary rights to inventions that are created by the founders and employees while they are working for the company, the company should enter into a *proprietary rights assignment of inventions agreement* with each of such individuals.

A proprietary rights assignment of inventions agreement elucidates what constitutes an invention, when the employee should disclose an invention, how the ownership is determined, and what the employee retains ownership of. The assignment should include any inventions made while employed by the company (so including inventions made at home or outside business hours). Very often, the assignment agreement is combined with a confidentiality agreement, defining the responsibilities of the employee with regard to confidential information.

If the assignment is included in an employment agreement, it should survive termination of the employment with the Company. Furthermore, attention should be paid to possible conflicts with earlier agreements that may still be in force. If, for example, a founder is also employed (on a part-time basis) by a university, entering into a proprietary rights assignment of inventions agreement with the company may conflict with his existing assignment arrangements with the university.

Assignment Inventions: Prior to Closing, each Founder and key employee will enter into a proprietary rights assignment agreement in a form reasonably acceptable to the Investors. Such agreement will contain, inter alia, appropriate terms and conditions under which each Founder and key employee will assign to the Company their relevant existing patents and patent applications and other intellectual property rights as defined by the Company's business plan. [In the event that a Founder is not allowed to assign his IP under any outstanding arrangement, as evidenced by such an arrangement, said Founders' requirement to assign his IP will be amended in a way acceptable to the Investors.

4.38 KEY MAN INSURANCE

As stated in *section 34 – Employment Relationships,* of this chapter, certain employees can be extremely important to the company. In case of any such employee being permanently unavailable, the company could be faced with a serious setback, which might lead to substantial negative financial consequences. By providing key employees with strong incentives by way of an ESOP, (see *section 30 – Employee Pool,* of this chapter); by seeing to it that adequate agreements are in place (containing, for example, non-compete clauses); and by locking in founders through a vesting scheme with good leaver and bad leaver provisions (see *section 31 – Vesting Scheme,* of this chapter) and a lock-up clause (see *section 33 – Lock-Up,* of this chapter), investors may minimise the risk of key employees or founders leaving (and thereby causing damage to) the company. These measures, however, cannot protect investors and the company against the possibility of such persons becoming incapacitated or passing away. By stipulating that the company purchase a life insurance policy for those members of the company's management who have been identified by the investors and the company as key members, the potential negative financial consequences upon the incapacitation or death of such a key member may be (partially) offset.

Most key man clauses determine that the company should be the beneficiary of the key man insurance. Such clauses however also usually state that the proceeds from such key man insurance can be used to redeem the shares of investors. In other words, in the event of the incapacitation or death of a key man, the key man insurance becomes a source of funds for redemption.

Key Man Insurance:	[Within [number] months of the Closing,] the Company will procure a life insurance policy for those individuals deemed to be key members of the Company's management team in the amount of €[__] million per person (or such lesser amount as approved by the Investors). [The Company will purchase such policies within [60] days after the Supervisory Board determines these key members of the team.] The Company will be named as the beneficiary of the policies [provided however that at the election of the holders of a [qualified] majority of the Series [●] Shares, such proceeds will be used to redeem Series [●] Shares].

4.39 AGREEMENTS AT CLOSING

In a venture capital financing, two essential agreements are used to document and govern investment terms and the relationship between the investors, the company and the other shareholders: the *investment (or subscription) agreement* and the *shareholders' agreement*. Sometimes these two agreements are combined in a single document.

The *investment agreement* contains the basic terms and conditions governing the investment. It includes a description of the securities issued and the purchase price thereof. It often also contains representations, warranties and covenants of the company and/or its founders. If the investment is payable in tranches, the investment agreement will also define the applicable timelines and milestones. The agreement will be entered into by the new investors, the company and the existing shareholders. Investment agreements are often referred to as *subscription agreements*, or *share* (or *stock*) *purchase agreements*.

A *shareholders' agreement* governs the rights and obligations of shareholders vis-à-vis each other and the company. It specifies the framework set out in the term sheet with respect to these rights and obligations. A shareholders' agreement usually contains many clauses that regulate the issuance and/or transfer of shares in the company and includes provisions that deal with the composition and duties of the management board and the supervisory board. It further stipulates the rights, preferences and restrictions associated with the holding of the preferred shares. The shareholders' agreement will be entered into by all shareholders and the company. The rights granted to the investors are sometimes set forth in a separate *investors' rights agreement*. Rights pertaining to a future public offering are often set forth (particularly in the U.S.) in a *registration rights agreement*. The company's articles of association or bylaws should be amended where necessary to be in conformity with the shareholders agreement. Insofar as that is not possible, the shareholders agreement should include adequate provisions ensuring that the terms and conditions of the shareholders agreement have priority over any deviating provisions of the company's articles or bylaws.

In addition to the investment agreement and shareholders' agreement, investors may also require that founders and key employees enter into new employment agreements, non-competition and non-solicitation agreements, non-disclosure agreements, and proprietary rights assignment agreements, all in a form reasonably acceptable to the investors (see *section 34 – Employment Relationships,* of this chapter).

Agreements at Closing:	The purchase of the Series [●] Shares will be made pursuant to a(n) [Investment Agreement][Subscription Agreement][Share Purchase Agreement][and Shareholders' Agreement] acceptable to the Investors and containing, inter alia, appropriate representations, warranties as referenced in the 'Representation and Warranties' clause and covenants of the Company, [Founder][Management Board][and existing shareholders], where appropriate, reflecting the provisions set forth herein and appropriate conditions of the Closing.

4.40 FEES AND EXPENSES

Venture capital investments are usually subject to a thorough internal and external *due diligence* investigation to assess the proposed valuation of the company and to ensure appropriate contractual coverage for risk items. The costs involved in conducting a due diligence are based on the scope and duration of the effort, which in turn are dependent on the complexity of the target business and other factors such as the type and number of external consultants involved. Investors view due diligence costs as a necessary expense that is justified by the clearer insight it gives them in all essential aspects of the company. On the one hand, this insight can enable investors to assist the company to benefit from opportunities with greater effectiveness, while on the other, it enables them to protect themselves contractually against perceived risks as well as to help the company mitigate its risks.

Before the incurring of costs or initiating of the due diligence and contract drafting process, the investors need to have clarity on who will bear the related expenses. Obviously, they will want them to be the responsibility of the company. Founders usually don't have a problem with the company bearing all the costs (sometimes capped to a certain amount) if the investors actually make the investment. The debate generally focuses on who should bear the costs if the term sheet does not result in an actual investment.

Fees and Expenses:	The Company will pay reasonable fees and expenses incurred by [name lead investor] in connection with (the preparation of) the transaction contemplated by this Term Sheet, including (but not limited to) expenses in connection with the preparation of legal documentation and the conduct of due diligence investigation(s) [subject to a cap of €[___]][payable at the Closing or payable as soon as the Company elects not to proceed with the transaction contemplated by this Term Sheet] [payable at the Closing or payable at the end of the exclusivity period if no transaction has occurred for whatever reason].

4.41 CONFIDENTIALITY

The *confidentiality* clause is generally quite straightforward. If investors and a company are seriously contemplating a transaction, it is usually in both their interests to agree to keep their negotiations and the information relating thereto confidential.

The confidentiality clause is one of the binding provisions of a term sheet. This means that parties may be held liable for damages incurred as a result of breach of this clause. Parties should therefore exercise great caution while agreeing to such a clause. Strangely enough, in practice these provisions are usually set out in very general terms, without indicating an expiration date or specifying events that do not fall within the scope of the confidentiality.

The confidentiality clause in a term sheet does not usually include a confidentiality undertaking by the parties with respect to information related to the company's technology, intellectual property and strategy disclosed to the investors in the course of their due diligence. Such information will normally be covered by a separate confidentiality arrangement executed between the company and the potential investor before the company sends out its business plan or other documents containing proprietary information.

Confidentiality: The parties will keep strictly confidential the fact that they have entered into negotiations concerning the transactions contemplated by this Term Sheet and the contents of such negotiations and of this Term Sheet. [After the expiry of [___] months after the date on which this Term Sheet is executed, the parties will no longer be bound by this confidentiality clause.]

4.42 EXCLUSIVITY/NO-SHOP

Once the term sheet has been signed, the investors will commence their due diligence process. During this due diligence phase investors investigate the business case of the company in great detail. In doing so, they typically involve external experts and therefore start incurring serious costs. Obviously, the investors would wish to avoid a situation wherein the company can inform them during the due diligence process that it has agreed to have other investors finance the company, thereby making the original investors redundant. Investors regard the signing of a term sheet as a serious indication of their intention to invest in a company. They are committed to pursuing that intention and expect a similar commitment from the company. By agreeing to an *exclusivity/no-shop clause*, the company can demonstrate to the investors that it is committed to entering into a transaction with the investors and will not (within a reasonable timeframe) explore the possibility of finding alternative investors to replace the original investors.

| **Exclusivity/ No-Shop:** | The Company agrees to work in good faith expeditiously towards the Closing. The Company agrees and shall ensure that the Founders, its key employees, its shareholders and the members of its corporate bodies agree (a) to discontinue any discussions with other parties concerning any investment in the Company, (b) not to take any action to solicit, initiate, encourage or assist the submission of any proposal, negotiation or offer from any person or entity other than the Investors relating to the sale or issuance, of any of the capital shares of the Company [or the acquisition, sale, lease, license or other disposition of the Company or any material part of the shares or assets of the Company] (c) to notify the Investors promptly of any inquiries by any third parties in regards to the foregoing. This provision 'Exclusivity/No-Shop' will be in force until [●].

[Thereafter this exclusivity period will automatically continue for a period of two weeks (revolving) unless either the Company or the Investors decide to end the discussions by way of a written notice to the other party at least five days prior to the ending of such exclusivity period.] |

4.43 GOVERNING LAW

The *governing law clause* is a standard clause in virtually every legal document. By including a clause stating the law that governs the agreement and applicable jurisdiction, future disagreements about these matters may be avoided. This is obviously in the interest of all parties to the agreement.

| **Governing Law:** | This Term Sheet and all other agreements resulting from this Term Sheet will be exclusively governed by [applicable law].

Insofar as permissible by law, exclusive jurisdiction for all disputes arising from and in connection with the present Term Sheet will be the seat of the Company. |

4.44 NON-BINDING CHARACTER

The *non-binding character clause* sets out the non-binding character of the term sheet. It is a summary of terms and consequently lacks many conditions and details one would normally want in the final agreements. A term sheet in fact functions as a *gentleman's agreement* binding the parties only psychologically and morally to the deal. It should move parties towards final (binding) documentation by reducing misunderstandings between the parties and by setting forth a time line for negotiations, including a deadline for closing.

From the founders' perspective, a non-binding term sheet provides an instrument to assess the seriousness of the investors' intentions in a non-binding fashion, and to determine at an early stage in the transaction, the economic and strategic advantages of the proposed deal. From the investor's perspective, it enables the investor to establish whether or not the proposed terms are acceptable to the company without immediately committing himself to the investment.

Nevertheless, despite the positive effects of a non-binding document, the investors will normally only pursue a transaction, enter into due diligence, involve external experts and make related costs, if certain conditions in the term sheet are legally binding and enforceable. Therefore, term sheets usually contain terms explicitly stated to be binding. These binding terms tend to deal not so much with the investment-related clauses but more with the regulation of the negotiation process, and include items such as exclusivity/no-shop, confidentiality, payment of fees and expenses, governing law, and indemnities.

Entering into a binding agreement regarding the exclusivity/no-shop and confidentiality clauses, gives the investor the confidence of knowing that the company is fully engaged and committed to the contemplated transaction and to the investor and is not shopping around for alternatives (see *section 42 – Exclusivity/No-Shop*, of this chapter) or disclosing deal specific information to the investor's competitors (see *section 41 – Confidentiality*, of this chapter). The allocation of expenses is another important issue that the investors normally want to include as a binding commitment. It assures the investor that he will get all or at least some of his expenses back, even if the deal does not materialise (see *section 40 – Fees and Expenses*, of this chapter). The clauses setting out the applicable law and indemnities are an instrument to assure that breach of any of these binding provisions is actually subject to legal enforcement.

In some jurisdictions, the court may hold that the parties are bound to the term sheet if it perceives that the parties clearly intended it to have some contractual effect, even if the term sheet itself clearly states that it is, apart from certain clauses, a non-binding document. In their evaluations, courts generally take into account the language of the term sheet, the substance and form of the communication during the term sheet negotiations and the (partial) performance of obligations under the term sheet. While drafting a term sheet, parties can take precautions that should decrease the chances of the term sheet being misconstrued. Two rules of thumb are: (i) clearly state that the term sheet is subject to the execution of a formal contract, as well as the fulfilment of other conditions precedent (see *section 46 – Conditions Precedent,* of this chapter); and (ii) avoid making the term sheet overly complex, legalistic or binding for a large proportion of its content. If a term sheet is too detailed, in some jurisdictions the court may hold that the parties have reached an agreement on all essential terms of the transaction, with only the mechanics and details left to be supplied by the parties.

Non-Binding Character:	Except as otherwise herein specifically provided, the parties to this Term Sheet expressly agree that no binding obligations will be created until a definitive agreement is executed with the requisite formality and delivered by both parties. Notwithstanding the foregoing, the 'Fees and Expenses', 'Confidentiality', 'Exclusivity/No-Shop', 'Governing Law' and 'Indemnities' clauses will be binding upon execution of this Term Sheet.

4.45 INDEMNITIES

As stated in the previous section (*Non-Binding Character*), the term sheet mainly has a non-binding character. Nevertheless, certain clauses of the term sheet are binding. It is therefore logical to determine that if one party to the term sheet breaches one of these binding clauses, it must indemnify the other party against all losses and damages resulting from such a breach.

In addition to indemnification in the afore-mentioned situations, the indemnification clause usually contains a provision dealing with finder's fees. The effect of such a provision is generally to ensure that any finder's fees that may be due in connection with the (proposed) investment in the company are borne by the party responsible for agreeing to such a finder's fee.

For example, let us assume a company were to engage an investment bank to find an investor who is willing to invest a certain amount in the company. Let's further assume the company were to agree to pay the investment bank a finder's fee in the case that it found such an investor and this investor subsequently were to invest the required amount in the company. By including a finder's fee clause in the term sheet, the investor would be entitled to subtract the value of the finder's fee (due by the company to the investment bank) from the value of the company when determining the value of the company (and thus the percentage of the shares that the investor will get in exchange for his investment in the company). By so doing, the investor would avoid in effect paying for a finder's fee to which not the investor, but the company had agreed.

Indemnities:	The Company and the Investors will each indemnify the other for any finder's fees for which either is responsible. The Company and the Investors will each indemnify the other against all losses and damages arising out of or relating to breach of the binding obligations: the 'Fees and Expenses' 'Confidentiality', 'Exclusivity/No-Shop', 'Governing Law' and 'Indemnities' clauses of this Term Sheet.

4.46 CONDITIONS PRECEDENT

The *conditions precedent clause* sets out the events that have to occur before the investors are willing to consummate the transaction. The period in which the conditions precedent need to be satisfied starts at execution of the term sheet and ends at the closing of the investment (see *section 9 – Anticipated Closing Date*, of this chapter). Most term sheets will contain conditions precedent dealing with the matters discussed below. Nevertheless, other conditions precedent may be included in the term sheet to meet specific requirements of the deal.

Investors execute a term sheet when they have made a preliminary decision to invest in the company. Under normal circumstances, such a decision is based on general information provided by the company (e.g. business plan and budget) and on the investors' specific expertise in the area in which the company operates. Before closing, the investors will try to verify whether the promises made and facts provided by the company are true and complete. This fact-finding process is called *due diligence investigation* (or simply *due diligence*). A due diligence is performed by or on behalf of the investors, with the purpose of identifying and minimising unnecessary risks prior to making their investment. Due diligence procedures usually concentrate around legal, financial, technological and business-related areas, but may – depending on the characteristics of each investment – also include more specific areas like the intellectual property, regulatory issues, market potential and strategy. The company and its founders are expected to co-operate with the investors or their consultants by disclosing to them all important information, requested or otherwise. Co-operation and disclosure may be included in the conditions precedent clause as a separate condition precedent.

Another condition that generally should be satisfied prior to closing is the *negotiation and execution of legal documentation* that is satisfactory to the investors and their legal counsel. The investors want to be sure that the final documentation reflects all clauses of the term sheet as well as the results of the pre-closing negotiations. These negotiations generally focus on interpretation of clauses in the term sheet and/or the due diligence results.

Most investors need the approval or recommendation of their investment committee or supervisory board before they are entitled to execute investment documentation. One of the most commonly seen conditions precedent therefore, is the investors' requirement to have final formal approval from their investment committee (or any other approving body).

An obvious condition precedent is the absence of a *material adverse change* (MAC) prior to closing. The financial condition and prospects of the company as set out in the business plan are the basis for the initial investment decision of the investors. They should therefore remain unchanged in the period after signing of the term sheet and in the foreseeable future (even after the closing date). The MAC clause is especially important when the actual signing of the legally binding documents and closing of the deal (see *section 9 – Anticipated Closing Date*, of this chapter) are on different dates.

The requirement to have the total amount of financing in place before the company is able to close the transaction is a prerequisite to the deal and is set out in a separate clause (see *section 2 – Amount of Financing*, of this chapter). Sometimes this condition is repeated as a condition precedent since its achievement is often the hardest to predict and fulfil in the period up to the anticipated closing date.

Under contract law, a condition precedent is a fact or event that must take place before there is a right to performance. If a term sheet is drafted as a binding document, the fulfilment of the conditions precedent will result in an obligation of the investor to fulfil his fiduciary duties by making the investment, and an obligation of the company to issue equity securities in exchange. However, since most term sheets are explicitly non-binding documents, the fulfilment of the conditions precedent will not automatically lead to an investment nor to the obligation to invest. The conditions precedent clause merely sets out the procedures that the investors will have to follow before they can execute legally binding investment documentation. It also functions as a benchmark to allow the investors to walk away elegantly from the deal, if, for example, the due diligence process does not bear out the truthfulness of the statement of affairs presented by the company.

If a condition precedent is not fulfilled, it provides the investors with grounds for termination of the proposed transaction or a basis for re-negotiation of the deal terms. If in such a case the investors nevertheless wish to pursue the investment contemplated in the term sheet, they may waive the condition precedent in question.

Conditions Precedent:	The Closing is subject to the following conditions precedent: (1) satisfactory completion of financial, [IP commercial, regulatory, tax] and legal due diligence; (2) no material adverse change in the financial condition or the prospects of the Company as mentioned in the business plan [and any documents sent to the Investors]; (3) negotiation and execution of legal documentation satisfactory to the Investors; (4) consent of the necessary legal majority of the Company's shareholders, and (5) final formal approval of the Investors' investment and partner committees.

4.47 EXPIRATION

The expiration date is the date on which the investor's offer as contained in the term sheet expires. By limiting the validity period of the term sheet, several purposes are served. First, the expiration feature limits the time during which the investor is (morally) bound by his offer. He can move on and concentrate on another investment opportunity in case of the present one not materialising. It further prevents the company from using the term sheet to negotiate deals with other investors. Sometimes the expiration exerts pressure upon the company to execute the term sheet and agree on the proposed terms within a reasonable time frame. It may also give the investor an early indication of the company's view on the transaction contemplated in the term sheet.

The period during which the term sheet should be valid, will be determined by the investor, by taking into consideration the above goals in relation to the peculiarities of each specific deal (e.g. competition by other investors, and complexity of the deal offered).

Expiration:	This Term Sheet expires on [date] if not accepted by the Company by that date.

ANNEXES

ANNEX 1: TERM SHEET TEMPLATE

Term sheet template also freely downloadable at www.venturecapitaldealterms.com

[NAME COMPANY]
SUMMARY OF PROPOSED TERMS AND CONDITIONS
SERIES [●] CONVERTIBLE PREFERRED SHARES

This term sheet (the "**Term Sheet**") summarises the principal terms and conditions with respect to the proposed investment by [name investor] in exchange for Series [●] Convertible Preferred Shares to be issued by [name company]

OFFERING TERMS

Issuer: [name company], (the "**Company**").

Amount of Financing: €[___] million (the "**Series [●] Financing**").

Milestones: [*Alternative 1: (investment milestone)*]: The Series [●] Financing is payable in [___] tranches of €[___] subject to the achievement of the milestones set forth in Appendix [___].]

[*Alternative 2: (valuation milestone)*]: The pre-money valuation of €[___] as referenced in the 'Share Price and Valuation' clause will be adjusted to €[___] subject to the achievement of the milestones set forth in Appendix [___].]

Investors:	[name investor] as lead investor will invest €[___]. Other investors participating in the Series [●] Financing (together with the lead investor, the "**Investors**"), the amounts of their investment to be approved by the lead investor.
Type of Security:	Series [●] convertible preferred shares (the "**Series [●] Shares**") are initially convertible on a 1:1 basis into the Company's common shares (the "**Common Shares**"). The Series [●] Shares and all other outstanding preferred shares (the "**Junior Preferred Shares**") are jointly referred to as the "**Preferred Shares**".
Warrant Coverage:	In addition to the Series [●] Shares, the Investors will also receive [___]% warrant coverage. For each Series [●] Share purchased, an Investor will receive a warrant to purchase [__] Common Shares/Series [●] Shares. The warrants will have a term expiring on the earlier of (i) [___] years from issuance or (ii) the date of completion of a Qualified Offering. The warrants will have standard anti-dilution protections. The warrants will be exercisable in cash or on a cash-less basis, at the option of the holder, at an exercise price of [Original Purchase Price] per share.
Share Price and Valuation:	[*Alternative 1*: €[___] per share (the "**Original Purchase Price**") representing a fully diluted pre-money valuation of €[___].]
	[*Alternative 2*: €[___] per share (the "**Original Purchase Price**"). The Original Purchase Price represents a fully diluted pre-money valuation of €[___] based on all outstanding Common Share equivalents, including options and warrants, at the time of the Closing and including (a) [___] new options as an increase to the option pool, as reflected in the capitalisation table attached as Appendix [___] and (b) the additional shares issuable to the holders of Junior Preferred Shares as a result of the anti-dilution protection in connection with the transaction contemplated in the Term Sheet.]

Capital Structure:	The attached capitalisation table (Appendix [___]) details all of the securities that will be outstanding immediately prior to and after the Closing.
Anticipated Closing Date:	[date] (the "**Closing**"). [provide for multiple closings if applicable].
Dividends:	The Series [●] Shares will carry a dividend in preference to the Common Shares of [___]% of the Original Purchase Price per annum, which will accrue and cumulate annually and will be payable only if declared.
	[The dividend will be payable in Series [●] Shares at the Original Purchase Price or in cash at the option of the Investors in the event of a liquidation or a Deemed Liquidation Event and without any compounding.]
	[Without the approval of the holders of a [qualified] majority of the Series [●] Shares, no dividends will be paid on the Common Shares or Junior Preferred Shares so long as Series [●] Shares are outstanding.]
Redemption:	At the election of the holders of at least [___]% of the Series [●] Shares, subject to any restrictions under applicable law, the Company will redeem (...)
	[*Alternative 1*: (...) all outstanding Series [●] Shares in full, at any time after the fifth anniversary of the Closing.]
	[*Alternative 2*: (...) one third of the outstanding Series [●] Shares on the fourth anniversary, one half of the outstanding Series [●] Shares on the fifth anniversary of the Closing and all of the remaining outstanding Series [●] Shares on the sixth anniversary of the Closing.]
	Such redemption will be at a purchase price equal to the Original Purchase Price (as adjusted for stock splits, stock dividends and the like) plus any accrued and unpaid dividends.

[In the event that the Company does not have funds legally available for such redemption, the Series [●] Shareholders will have the right to require the Company to take any further steps necessary to effect a sale of the Company, including retention of an investment banker appointed by the Series [●] Shareholders to actively market the Company for sale to a third party.]

Voluntary Conversion: A holder of Series [●] Shares will have the right to convert Series [●] Shares, or any part of such shares including declared dividends, at the option of the holder, at any time, into Common Shares. The total number of Common Shares into which each Series [●] Share may be converted will be determined by dividing the Original Purchase Price by the conversion price. The conversion price will initially be equal to the Original Purchase Price. The conversion price will however be subject to a proportional adjustment for share dividends, splits, combinations and similar events and in accordance with the 'Anti-Dilution' clause.

[*Milestone*: the conversion price of the Series [●] Shares will be adjusted to €[___] per share if the Company fails to meet any of the milestones set forth in Appendix [___] to this Term Sheet.]

Automatic Conversion: The Series [●] Shares, including declared dividends, and all other Preferred Shares will automatically be converted into Common Shares at the then applicable conversion price upon (i) the closing of a firmly underwritten public offering with a price per Common Share of at least [___] times the Original Purchase Price (subject to adjustments for share dividends, splits, combinations and similar events) and [net/gross] proceeds to the Company of not less than €[___] (a "**Qualified Offering**"), or (ii) upon the written consent of the holders of (a) [___]% of the Series [●] Shares, voting separately [and (b) [___]% of the Preferred Shares of the Company, voting together as a single class.

Anti-Dilution: In the event that the Company issues new shares, or securities convertible into or exchangeable for shares, at a purchase price lower than the applicable conversion price of the Series [●] Shares, then the conversion price of the Series [●] Shares will be subject to a(n) (...)

[*Alternative 1*: (...) full ratchet adjustment, reducing the applicable conversion price of the Series [●] Shares to the price at which the new shares are (to be) issued.]

[*Alternative 2*: (...) [broad based][narrow based] weighted average adjustment, reducing the applicable conversion price of the Series [●] Shares to a new conversion price calculated in accordance with a weighted average anti-dilution formula.]

[*Alternative 3*: (...) full ratchet adjustment within [____] years of the Closing. Thereafter, the conversion price will be subject to adjustment on a [broad based][narrow based] weighted-average basis.]

[*Alternative 4*: (...) (a) [broad based] [narrow based] weighted-average adjustment if the purchase price per share is equal to or greater than €[____] per share and (b) full ratchet adjustment if the purchase price per share is lower than €[____] per share.]

[*Alternative 5*: (...) adjustment, reducing the applicable conversion price of the Series [●] Shares to a new conversion price calculated as the average of the conversion prices resulting from the weighted average adjustment and the full ratchet adjustment (new conversion price = (WA + FR)/2).]

[In the event that the Company issues new shares, or securities convertible into or exchangeable for shares, at a purchase price lower than the applicable purchase price of the Series [●] Shares, the holders of Series [●] Shares may elect that the Company shall procure (to the extent that it is lawfully able to do so) the issue to the holders of Series [●] Shares, additional Series [●] Shares against payment of such an amount that the average purchase price they have paid is equal to the purchase price at which the new shares are issued.]

The anti-dilution adjustment will not apply in the event of issuance of (...)

[*Alternative 1*: (...) Common Shares issued or issuable to employees, consultants or directors of the Company directly or pursuant to the ESOP (as set out in the 'Employee Pool' clause) that have been approved by the Supervisory Board.].

[*Alternative 2*: (...) (i) Common Shares issued or issuable to employees, consultants or directors of the Company directly or pursuant to the ESOP (as set out in the 'Employee Pool' clause) that have been approved by the Supervisory Board; (ii) Common Shares issued or issuable upon conversion of the Preferred Shares; (iii) Common Shares issued or issuable in connection with a merger, acquisition, combination, consolidation or other reorganisation involving the Company and approved by the Supervisory Board of the Company; (iv) Common Shares issued or issuable in connection with (a) any borrowings from a commercial lending institution, (b) the lease of equipment or property by the Company, or (c) strategic partnerships and/or licensing relationships, so long as such transactions are approved by the Supervisory Board; and (v) Common Shares issued or issuable (a) in a public offering before or in connection with which all outstanding Preferred Shares will be converted to Common Shares or (b) upon exercise of warrants or rights granted to underwriters in connection with such a public offering.]

Pay-to-Play: Holders of Preferred Shares are required to participate in any dilutive issuance [including the Series [●] Financing] to the extent of their pro rata equity interest in the Preferred Shares, [unless the participation requirement is waived for all Preferred Shareholders by the Supervisory Board [(including the Series [●] Director)]][unless the holders of [●]% of the Series [●] Shares elect otherwise].

In the event that a holder of Preferred Shares fails to participate in accordance with the previous paragraph, the Preferred Shares held by such shareholder will automatically [and proportionally], [lose their anti-dilution rights][lose their liquidation rights][convert to Common Shares].

Liquidation Preference: In the event of a liquidation or winding up of the Company, the holders of Series [●] Shares will be entitled to receive in preference to the holders of Junior Preferred Shares and the holders of Common Shares payment of an amount equal to [___ times] the Original Purchase Price per Series [●] Share [plus any accumulated and unpaid dividends].

If there are insufficient assets or proceeds to pay such amount to the holders of Series [●] Shares in full, the amount available will be paid on a pro rata basis between the holders of Series [●] Shares.

Thereafter, the holders of Junior Preferred Shares will receive payment in full of the original purchase price paid per Junior Preferred Share [plus any accumulated and unpaid dividends].

[*Alternative 1: (non-participating liquidation preference):* Thereafter, any remaining assets or proceeds will be paid exclusively to the holders of Common Shares on a pro rata basis.]

[*Alternative 2: (participating liquidation preference)*]: Thereafter, any remaining assets or proceeds will be distributed pro rata among the holders of Common Shares and the holders of Preferred Shares (the latter on an as-if converted basis).]

[*Alternative 3 (non-participating with conversion at the option of investor)*: In the event of a liquidation (...), the holders of Series [●] Shares will be entitled to receive, in preference to the holders of common shares, an amount equal to the greater of (i) the Original Subscription Price of the Series [●] Shares held plus any accrued and unpaid dividends and (ii) the amount they would have received had they converted the Series [●] Shares to common shares immediately prior to such liquidation or winding up.]

[*Alternative 4: (capped participating liquidation preference)*: Thereafter, any remaining assets or proceeds will be distributed pro rata among the holders of Common Shares and the holders of Preferred Shares (the latter on an as-if converted basis) until such time that the holders of Series [●] Preferred Shares have received an aggregate of [___ times] the Original Purchase Price per share (including any amounts paid pursuant to the paragraphs above). The balance thereafter will be distributed amongst the holders of Common Shares on a pro rata basis.]

A reorganisation, consolidation, merger of the Company, sale or issue of Shares or any other event pursuant to which the shareholders of the Company will have less than 51% of the voting power of the surviving or acquiring corporation, or the sale, lease, transfer or other disposition of all or substantially all of the Company's assets will be deemed to be a liquidation or winding up for the purposes of the liquidation preference (a "**Deemed Liquidation Event**"), thereby triggering the liquidation preferences described above [unless the holders of [___]% of the Series [●] Shares elect otherwise].

Favourable Terms: The terms herein, other than valuation, are subject to a review of the rights, preferences and restrictions pertaining to the existing shares in the Company. Any changes necessary to conform such existing shares to this Term Sheet will be made at the Closing as necessary in order to ensure that holders of existing Common Shares and Junior Preferred Shares will not have rights more favourable than those of the holders of Series [●] Shares.

Board Representation: The supervision of the policies by the Management Board and all other tasks and duties as assigned to it will be entrusted to the supervisory board (the "**Supervisory Board**"), which at Closing will consist of [___] members comprised of (i) [___] member(s) elected upon the nomination of the holders of a [qualified] majority of the Series [●] Shares (the "**Series [●] Director**"), (ii) [___] member(s) elected upon the nomination of the holders of the Preferred Shares, (iii) [___] elected upon the nomination of [[ ] (the "**Founders**")], and (iv) [___] person(s) who have specific expertise in the Company's field of business elected by a [qualified] majority of all shareholders and who are mutually acceptable [to the Founders and Investors][to the other directors].

[In addition, [name(s) Investor(s)][so long as it [they] hold(s) at least [___]% of the [Series [●] Shares] [outstanding shares] will have the right to designate one observer to the Supervisory Board, who will have the right to participate in discussions and to receive information, but will not be entitled to vote.]

The Supervisory Board will meet at least [quarterly] with intermittent teleconferencing for at least the first [twelve (12)] months after Closing.

The Company will pay the reasonable expenses incurred by members of the Supervisory Board in attending Supervisory Board meetings, including committee meetings, or otherwise representing the Company. Furthermore, [___] will receive an annual retainer of €[___] and a per-meeting fee of €[___].

[Following the Closing, the Supervisory Board will establish an audit committee and a compensation committee to be composed of the Series [●] Director and [___]. The compensation committee will be responsible for reviewing and approving all option grants, as well as compensation of officers of the Company and all non-officer employees whose annual salary exceeds €[___].]

The Company will [maintain][take out] D&O insurance in the amount of at least €[five (5)] million per occurrence.

Voting Rights: The holders of Series [●] Shares will vote together with the holders of Common Shares and not as a separate class except as specifically provided herein or as otherwise required by law. [Each Series [●] Share will have a number of votes equal to the number of Common Shares issuable upon conversion of such Series [●] Share.] [Each Series [●] Share and Common Share will have one vote.]

Consent Rights: [*Alternative 1*: The Company's articles of association or any other constitutive corporate documents will be amended to contain restrictions making certain resolutions of the Management Board with a material effect on the Company's operations or management subject to the prior approval of the Supervisory Board and/or the holders of [Preferred Shares][Series [●] Shares], as the case may be. In addition, these documents will contain restrictions making certain resolutions of the general meeting of shareholders (e.g. resolutions regarding the structure and capitalisation of the Company) [subject to the prior approval of the holders of [Preferred Shares][Series [●] Shares][subject to a qualified majority of votes].]

[*Alternative 2*: The approval of a [qualified] majority of the Supervisory Board [including the Series [●] Director] and/or the holders of [Preferred Shares][Series [●] Shares] and/or a qualified majority of [two thirds/three fourths] of the votes in the general meeting will be required for the following actions [unless provided for in the annual budget]: (i) engagement in any new line of business or jurisdiction where the Company is managed and controlled or any material modification of the business plan; (ii) approval of the annual budget and any non-budgeted expenses in excess of €[___]; (iii) implementation of an Employee Stock Option Plan and granting any rights thereunder; (iv) appointment of employees with a yearly salary in excess of €[___]; (v) disposal or acquisition of any securities in the capital of any other company or establishment of any new branch or subsidiary of the Company; (vi) exercise of voting rights in the shareholders' meeting of any subsidiary or affiliate, if any; (vii) conduct of any litigation on behalf of the Company; (viii) entering into a guarantee or indemnity or otherwise committing the Company (other than in the ordinary course of business); (ix) provision of any loan or advance or any credit (other than in the ordinary course of business) to any person;

(x) entering into any transactions with related parties; (xi) changing the accounting policies; (xii) entering into any agreements, contracts or arrangements that are not of an at arm's length nature; and (xiii) undertaking any such legal acts as will be determined and clearly defined by the Supervisory Board and notified to the Management Board in writing.

The approval of a [qualified] majority of the [Preferred Shares voting together as a class][Series [●] Shares] and/or a qualified majority of [two thirds/three fourths] of the votes in the general meeting will be required for the following actions:

(i) issuance of any securities (including instruments convertible into securities and the issuance of subordinated debt); (ii) declaration and/or payment of any and all dividends by the Company; (iii) entering into any merger, consolidation, recapitalisation, change of control, or sale of all or substantially all of the assets of the Company; (iv) undertaking of any filing for bankruptcy, insolvency by or against the Company; (v) engagement in any transaction that constitutes a deemed dividend according to the relevant tax laws; and (vi) making of any amendments to the articles of association/charter/bylaws of the Company that adversely impact the [Preferred Shares][Series [●] Shares], including by way of merger, consolidation or otherwise.

Registration Rights: [*Alternative* 1: The holders of [Preferred Shares][Series [●] Shares] will have normal registration rights including demand registration rights, [unlimited] 'piggyback' registration rights, S-3 registration rights, transfer of registration rights, proportionate underwriter cutbacks, and other typical registration rights, all at the expense of the Company. The registration rights of all [Preferred Shares][Series [●] Shares] will be the same.]

[*Alternative 2*: All Common Shares [issued or] to be issued upon conversion of the [Preferred Shares][Series [●] Shares] will be deemed "**Registrable Securities**".

Demand Registration: Upon the earliest of (i) [three-five] years after the Closing; or (ii) [six] months following an initial public offering ("**IPO**"), persons holding [30-50]% of the Registrable Securities may request [one][two] (consummated) registrations of their shares by the Company. The aggregate offering price for such registration may not be less than €[___] million. In the event of any cut-backs by the Company and/or its underwriters, shares to be registered by holders of Registrable Securities will have first priority for registration.

Registration on Form S-3: The holders of [10-30]% of the Registrable Securities will have the right to require the Company to register on Form S-3 (if available for use by the Company) Registrable Securities for an aggregate offering price of at least €[___] million. There will be no limit on the aggregate number of such Form S-3 registrations, provided that there are no more than [two] per year.

Piggyback Registration: The holders of Registrable Securities will be entitled to 'piggyback' registration rights on all registration statements of the Company, subject to the right, however, of the Company and its underwriters to reduce the number of shares proposed to be registered to a minimum of [30]% on a pro rata basis and to complete reduction on an IPO at the underwriter's discretion. In all events, the shares to be registered by holders of Registrable Securities will be reduced only after all other shareholders' shares are reduced.

Transfer of registration rights: The registration rights may be transferred to a transferee (other than to a competitor of the Company) who acquires at least €[___] of the shares held by a holder of [Preferred Shares][Series [●] Shares]. [Transfer of registration rights to a group company of any Investor will be without restriction with regards to minimum shareholding.] *Expenses*: The registration expenses (exclusive of share transfer taxes, underwriting discounts and commissions) will be borne by the Company. The Company will also pay the reasonable fees and expenses [not to exceed €___,] of one special counsel to represent all the participating shareholders.

Other registration provisions: Other provisions will be contained in the registration rights agreement with respect to registration rights as are reasonable, including cross-indemnification, the Company's ability to delay the filing of the demand registration for a period of not more than 120 days, the agreement by holders of [Preferred Shares][Series [●] Shares] if requested by the underwriter in a public offering not to sell any unregistered shares they hold for a period of up to 120 days following the effective date of the Registration Statement of such offering, the period of time during which the Registration Statement will be kept effective, underwriting arrangements and the like. [The registration rights will apply exclusively to Common Shares issued upon conversion of [Preferred Shares][Series [●] Shares] and the Company will have no obligation to register an offering of any other shares.]

If so requested by the managing underwriter, the holders of Preferred Shares will reach an agreement with regard to the IPO not to sell or transfer any Common Shares of the Company [(excluding shares acquired in or following the IPO)] for a period of up to 180 days following the IPO (provided all directors and officers of the Company and [1 – 5]% shareholders agree to the same lock-up).]

[In the event that the public offering as referred to in this 'Registration Rights' clause will or has taken place on a stock exchange outside the U.S., then the holders of Registrable Securities will be entitled to registration rights equivalent to the rights and obligations contained in this 'Registration Rights' clause (or as equivalent as possible given differences in applicable law).]

Representations and Warranties: The investment agreement or a separate representation and warranties agreement will include standard representations and warranties granted by the [Company][Founder][Management Board][and existing shareholders], [including, but not expressly limited to: (i) organisation and good standing; (ii) capitalisation structure; (iii) due authorisation; (iv) valid share issuance; (v) governmental consents; (vi) no company litigation; (vii) ownership or exclusive license of intellectual property rights; (viii) employees; (ix) pension plans; (x) assurances of full disclosure and accuracy of information provided; (xi) good title to all assets; (xii) tax; (xiii) accuracy of financial statements; (xiv) absence of adverse developments; and (xv) material contracts].

Information Rights: [Any holder of Series [●] Shares][As long as the holders of [Preferred Shares][Series [●] Shares] [(provided that they are not a competitor of the Company)] continue to hold at least [___] [Preferred Shares][Series [●] Shares], they] will be granted access to the Company facilities and personnel during normal business hours and with reasonable advance notification. The Company will deliver to such shareholder(s) (i) un-audited financial statements within 120 days after the end of the calendar year; (ii) quarterly [and monthly] financial statements within 20 days after such period, and other information as determined by the Supervisory Board; (iii) thirty days prior to the end of each fiscal year, a comprehensive operating budget forecasting the Company's revenues, expenses, and cash position on a month-to-month basis for the upcoming fiscal year; and (iv) promptly following the end of each quarter, an up-to-date capitalisation table, certified by the CFO. The foregoing provisions will terminate upon a Qualified Offering.

Use of Proceeds: The Company will apply the net proceeds of the sale of the Series [●] Shares to the Investors exclusively to the development and operation of the Company in accordance with a business plan (including key milestones) and a twelve month budget to be [agreed upon by the Company and the Investors][approved by the Investors] prior to Closing.

Pre-Emptive Rights: Without prejudice to the 'Anti-Dilution' clause, if the Company proposes to offer equity securities, or securities convertible into or exchangeable for shares, the holders of [Preferred Shares][Series [●] Shares] will be entitled to purchase (…)

[*Alternative 1*: (...) on a pro rata basis all or any portion of such securities. Any securities not subscribed for by a holder of [Preferred Shares][Series [●] Shares] may be reallocated among the other holders of [Preferred Shares][Series [●] Shares]. If holders of [Preferred Shares][Series [●] Shares] do not purchase all of such securities, the portion that is not purchased may be offered to the other shareholders on terms not less favourable to the Company for a period of [60] days.]

[*Alternative 2*: (...) such securities in an amount sufficient to allow the holders of [Preferred Shares][Series [●] Shares] to retain their fully diluted ownership of the Company.]

[The pre-emptive right will not apply in the event of issuances of (i) Common Shares issued or issuable to employees, consultants or directors of the Company directly or pursuant to the ESOP (as set out in the 'Employee Pool' clause) that have been approved by the Supervisory Board; (ii) Common Shares issued or issuable upon conversion of the Preferred Shares; (iii) Common Shares issued or issuable in connection with a merger, acquisition, combination, consolidation or other reorganisation involving the Company approved by the Supervisory Board of the Company; (iv) Common Shares issued or issuable in connection with (a) any borrowings from a commercial lending institution, (b) the lease of equipment or property by the Company, or (c) strategic partnerships and/or licensing relationships, so long as such transactions are approved by the Supervisory Board; and (v) Common Shares issued or issuable (a) in a public offering before or in connection with which all outstanding Preferred Shares will be converted to Common Shares or (b) upon exercise of warrants or rights granted to underwriters in connection with such a public offering.]

Rights of First Refusal: [Holders of [Preferred Shares][Series [●] Shares]][The Company first and holders of [Preferred Shares][Series [●] Shares] second *(or vice versa)*] have a right of first refusal with respect to any [share(s) in the Company] [Common Share(s)][and securities convertible into or exchangeable for shares] proposed to be sold by [a shareholder][Founder][and employees holding more than [1]% of the outstanding Common Shares (assuming conversion of the Preferred Shares)], at the same price and on the same terms as offered, with a right of over-subscription for holders of [Preferred Shares][Series [●] Shares] of [share(s) in the Company][Common Share(s)] [and securities convertible into or exchangeable for shares] un-subscribed by the other holders of [Preferred Shares][Series [●] Shares].

The right of first refusal will not apply in the event of (i) a transfer of shares approved by a majority of [75]% of the voting rights; or (ii) a transfer by a holder of Preferred Shares to an affiliate.

Such right of first refusal will terminate upon the earlier of [(i) ten years from the Closing Date;] (ii) a Qualified Offering; (iii) a sale or merger of the Company; [(iv) with respect to any employee, when such employee no longer owns any Common Shares]; [(v) with respect to any holder of [Preferred Shares][Series [●] Shares], when such holder of [Preferred Shares][Series [●] Shares] no longer owns at least [___] [Preferred Shares][Series [●] Shares]].

Co-Sale Right: Before any shareholder may sell its shares in the Company, after having observed the terms and procedures of the 'Right of first Refusal' clause, he will give [the other Shareholder] [the holder of [Preferred Shares] [Series [●] Shares] an opportunity to participate in such sale on a pro rata basis.

Drag-Along Right:	[*Alternative 1*: The holders of a [qualified] majority of the [Preferred Shares][Series [●] Shares] may require a sale of the entire issued share capital of the Company.]
	[*Alternative 2*: In the event, [that a third party makes an offer to acquire all of the outstanding shares of the Company][of a Deemed Liquidation Event], that is accepted by the holders of a [qualified] majority of the [Preferred Shares][Series [●] Shares], the other shareholders will be obliged to [vote in favour of such Deemed Liquidation Event and to take all actions necessary in connection therewith][offer their shares to said third party under the same terms and conditions specified in such offer] and accordingly (to the extent necessary) waive their rights of first refusal etc.]
	[If the holders of the [Preferred Shares][Series [●] Shares] wish to exercise the drag-along right as set out in the previous paragraph within [___] years after the Closing, the additional approval of the holders of a [qualified] majority of the outstanding Common Shares (assuming conversion of the Preferred Shares), will be required.]
Management Board:	The management of the Company will be entrusted to the management board (the "**Management Board**") consisting at Closing of [___] as chief executive officer and [___] as chief [ ] officer. Any new Management Board members or senior company officers will not receive an offer of employment without the approval of the Supervisory Board [including the Series [●] Director]. [The Company will, on a best-efforts basis, hire a chief [___] officer within the [six (6)] month period following the Closing.]

Employee Pool: Upon the Closing, the Company will reserve up to [[number of shares] Common Shares][[___]% of the post-money outstanding shares] for issuance to employees, directors and consultants (the "**Reserved Employee Shares**") [including the Common Shares presently reserved for issuance upon the exercise of outstanding options]. The Reserved Employee Shares will be issued from time to time under [such arrangements, contracts or plans][an employee share option plan (the "**ESOP**")] as [recommended by the Management Board and] approved by the Supervisory Board.

Vesting Scheme: All Reserved Employee Shares will be subject to vesting as follows: [25]% to vest at the end of the first year following their issuance, with the remaining [75]% to vest monthly over the next [three] years. Good leaver/bad leaver provisions will apply.

Founders' Shares: Upon the Closing, [number of shares] of the Company's issued and outstanding Common Shares will be held by the Founders (the "**Founders' Shares**"). The Founders' Shares will be subject to a similar vesting scheme as set forth in the 'Vesting Scheme' clause, provided that the vesting period will begin as of the Closing. [In addition, in the event that the Company milestones are not satisfied, the Company will have the right upon termination of employment of a Founder with or without cause, to repurchase his vested Founders' Shares in the Company at fair market value (as determined by the Supervisory Board).]

Lock-Up: At no time prior to [date] will any Founder or key employee, if any, dispose of any shares in the Company in any manner, except with the written consent of [two-thirds] of the holders of Series [●] Shares. This lock-up will in any case lapse at the consummation of a Qualified IPO, trade sale or other liquidity event.

Employment Relationships:	The Company has or will have prior to the Closing employment agreements in a form reasonably acceptable to the Investors with [the following persons: [names]][each Founder and key employee].
Non-Competition/Non-Solicitation:	Prior to Closing, each Founder and key employee will enter into a [one] year non-competition and non-solicitation agreement in a form reasonably acceptable to the Investors.
Non-Disclosure Agreement:	Prior to Closing, each current and former Founder, and each officer, employee and consultant with access to the Company's confidential information/trade secrets will enter into a non-disclosure agreement in a form reasonably acceptable to the Investors.
Assignment Inventions:	Prior to Closing, each Founder and key employee will enter into a proprietary rights assignment agreement in a form reasonably acceptable to the Investors. Such agreement will contain, *inter alia*, appropriate terms and conditions under which each Founder and key employee will assign to the Company their relevant existing patents and patent applications and other intellectual property rights as defined by the Company's business plan. [In the event that a Founder is not allowed to assign his IP under any outstanding arrangement, as evidenced by such an arrangement, said Founders' requirement to assign his IP will be amended in a way acceptable to the Investors.]

Key Man Insurance: [Within [number] months of the Closing,] the Company will procure a life insurance policy for those individuals deemed to be key members of the Company's management team in the amount of €[] million per person (or such lesser amount as approved by the Investors). [The Company will purchase such policies within [60] days after the Supervisory Board determines these key members of the team.] The Company will be named as the beneficiary of the policies [provided however that at the election of the holders of a [qualified] majority of the Series [●] Shares, such proceeds will be used to redeem Series [●] Shares].

Agreements at Closing: The purchase of the Series [●] Shares will be made pursuant to a(n) [Investment Agreement] [Subscription Agreement] [Share Purchase Agreement] [and Shareholders' Agreement] acceptable to the Investors and containing, inter alia, appropriate representations, warranties as referenced in the 'Representation and Warranties' clause and covenants of the Company, [Founder] [Management Board] [and existing shareholders], where appropriate reflecting the provisions set forth herein and appropriate conditions of the Closing.

Fees and Expenses: The Company will pay reasonable fees and expenses incurred by [name lead investor] in connection with (the preparation of) the transaction contemplated by this Term Sheet, including (but not limited to) expenses in connection with the preparation of legal documentation and the conduct of due diligence investigation(s) [subject to a cap of €[___]][payable at the Closing or payable as soon as the Company elects not to proceed with the transaction contemplated by this Term Sheet] [payable at the Closing or payable at the end of the exclusivity period if no transaction has occurred for whatever reason].

**Confiden-
tiality:**

The parties will keep strictly confidential the fact that they have entered into negotiations concerning the transactions contemplated by this Term Sheet and the contents of such negotiations and of this Term Sheet. [After the expiry of [___] months after the date on which this Term Sheet is executed, the parties will no longer be bound by this confidentiality clause.]

**Exclusivity/
No-Shop:**

The Company agrees to work in good faith expeditiously towards the Closing. The Company agrees and shall ensure that the Founders, its key employees, its shareholders and the members of its corporate bodies agree (a) to discontinue any discussions with other parties concerning any investment in the Company, (b) not to take any action to solicit, initiate, encourage or assist the submission of any proposal, negotiation or offer from any person or entity other than the Investors relating to the sale or issuance, of any of the capital shares of the Company [or the acquisition, sale, lease, license or other disposition of the Company or any material part of the shares or assets of the Company] (c) to notify the Investors promptly of any inquiries by any third parties in regards to the foregoing. This provision 'Exclusivity/No-Shop' will be in force until [●].

[Thereafter this exclusivity period will automatically continue for a period of two weeks (revolving) unless either the Company or the Investors decide to end the discussions by way of a written notice to the other party at least five days prior to the ending of such exclusivity period.]

**Governing
Law:**

This Term Sheet and all other agreements resulting from this Term Sheet will be exclusively governed by [applicable law].

Insofar as permissible by law, exclusive jurisdiction for all disputes arising from and in connection with the present Term Sheet will be the seat of the Company.

Non-Binding Character:	Except as otherwise herein specifically provided, the parties to this Term Sheet expressly agree that no binding obligations will be created until a definitive agreement is executed with the requisite formality and delivered by both parties.
  Notwithstanding the foregoing, the 'Fees and Expenses', 'Confidentiality', 'Exclusivity/No-Shop', 'Governing Law' and 'Indemnities' clauses will be binding upon execution of this Term Sheet.
Indemnities:	The Company and the Investors will each indemnify the other for any finder's fees for which either is responsible. [The Company and the Investors will each indemnify the other against all losses and damages arising out of or relating to breach of the binding obligations: the 'Fees and Expenses' 'Confidentiality', 'Exclusivity/No-Shop', 'Governing Law' and 'Indemnities' clauses of this Term Sheet.]
Conditions Precedent:	The Closing is subject to the following conditions precedent:
  (1) satisfactory completion of financial, [IP commercial, regulatory, tax] and legal due diligence; (2) no material adverse change in the financial condition or the prospects of the Company as mentioned in the business plan [and any documents sent to the Investors]; (3) negotiation and execution of legal documentation satisfactory to the Investors; (4) consent of the necessary legal majority of the Company's shareholders, and (5) final formal approval of the Investors' investment and partner committees.
Expiration:	This Term Sheet expires on [date] if not accepted by the Company by that date.

Signatures:

[Name Company]
Name: ....
Title: ....
Date: ....

[Name Founder(s)]	**[Name Investor(s)]**
Name:	Name: ....
Title:	Title: ....
Date:	Date: ....

ANNEX 2: PROFIT AND LOSS ACCOUNT AND CASH FLOW STATEMENT CASE STUDY

in k€	Seed	Series A	Series B	Series C	IPO	Post IPO
Profit & Loss						
Revenues						
Sales			2,000	40,000	90,000	150,000
Licensing		1,500	4,000	10,000	20,000	40,000
Cost of goods sold			-1,000	-20,000	-45,000	-75,000
Gross Margin	-	1,500	5,000	30,000	65,000	115,000
Research & development						
Prototype development	250	1,500	5,000	8,000	9,000	9,000
Production setup		500	2,500	3,000	3,500	3,500
Lab costs	250	750	2,000	3,500	4,000	4,000
Labor	200	1,000	4,000	4,500	5,000	5,000
Overhead						
Employment	100	1,000	2,000	3,000	3,500	3,500
Office costs	20	150	500	750	900	900
Marketing & sales	10	250	1,000	1,500	2,000	2,000
Legal & advisory	30	200	500	1,200	1,500	1,500
Patents	50	200	400	500	600	600
Other	10	200	400	500	750	750
Total expenses	920	5,750	18,300	26,450	30,750	30,750
EBIT	-920	-4,250	-13,300	3,550	34,250	84,250
Cash flow						
EBIT	-920	-4,250	-13,300	3,550	34,250	84,250
Working capital movement		-250	-550	-11,000	-24,750	-23,750
Capital expenditures	-500	-2,000	-5,000	-30,000	-5,000	-5,000
	-1,420	-6,500	-18,850	-37,450	4,500	55,500
Opening balance Cash	-	80	1,580	2,730	5,280	84,780
Operating cash flow	-1,420	-6,500	-18,850	-37,450	4,500	55,500
Financing	1,500	8,000	20,000	40,000	75,000	
Ending balance Cash	80	1,580	2,730	5,280	84,780	140,280
Accumulated cash flow	-1,420	-7,920	-26,770	-64,220	-59,720	-4,220
Valuation (pre-money)	2,500	15,000	45,000	100,000	200,000	

ANNEX 3: GLOSSARY OF TERMS

Accelerated vesting — a speeding up of the vesting schedule, for example in case of an exit.

Angel — a wealthy individual who invests in companies in relatively early stages of development.

Anti-dilution protection — a clause that protects an investor from a reduction in the value of his shares due to the issuance by the company of additional shares to other entities at a per share price that is lower than the per share price paid by the investor. The protection consists of an adjustment mechanism called a Ratchet.

Bridge loan — a short-term loan that will eventually be replaced by permanent capital from equity investors or debt lenders. In venture capital, a bridge loan is usually a short-term note (six to twelve months) that converts to preferred stock. See chapter 4, section 5 – Type of Security.

Broad-based weighted average — a system used in connection with anti-dilution protection. A broad-based weighted average protection adjusts downward the price per share of the preferred stock of investor A due to the issuance of new preferred shares to a new investor B at a price lower than the price investor A originally paid. Investor A's preferred stock is re-priced to a weighted average of investor A's price and investor B's price. If a broad-based weighted average system is used, the denominator of the formula for determining the new weighted average price contains the total number of outstanding common shares (on an as-if converted basis) on a fully diluted basis (including all convertible securities, warrants and options). See chapter 4, section 14 – Anti-Dilution.

Burn rate — the rate at which a company uses up its available funds (normally in order to meet its growth targets and cover its expenses). The burn rate is usually expressed on a monthly or weekly basis

Business plan — a document that describes a business opportunity and the manner in which such an opportunity can be transformed into a successful business. A business plan typically includes the following chapters: executive summary, product, management team, marketing plan, business system and organisation, realisation schedule, risks and financing.

Capitalisation table — a table providing an overview of the company's equity securities and, if any such securities have been issued, non-equity securities that can be converted into equity securities. The capitalisation (or cap) table usually also provides an overview of the owners of the aforementioned securities.

Capital gains — investment earnings resulting from the purchase and sale of shares or other assets.

Conversion — the converting of an investor's preferred shares into common shares at a pre-set conversion ratio, see chapter 4, section 12 – Voluntary Conversion; or the conversion of convertible notes into preferred shares at a conversion ratio based on the issue price of a future financing round, see chapter 4, section 5 – Type of Security.

Convertible note — a loan that allows the lender to exchange the debt for preferred shares in a company at a conversion ratio based on the issue price of a future financing round.

Convertible preferred shares — a type of shares that give the owner the right to convert such preferred shares to common shares. Convertible preferred shares are the most common type of equity used by venture capital investors to invest in companies. See chapter 4, section 5 – Type of Security.

Co-sale right — a right that enables an investor to include his shares in any sale by another shareholder at the same price and under the same terms and conditions that apply to the other shareholder. Also referred to as a Tag-along right.

Covenant — a legal promise to do or not do a certain thing.

Crowdfunding — the practice of funding a company by raising many small amounts of money from a large number of individuals, usually via the internet, based on a donation, rewards, lending or equity model.

Cumulative dividends — dividends that accrue. If a company cannot pay a cumulative dividend when it is due, it is still responsible for paying it in the future. The company must fulfil this obligation before it can pay out dividends to holders of any other classes of stock. See chapter 4, section 10 – Dividends.

Default — a company's failure to comply with the terms and conditions of a financing arrangement.

Demand registration — a type of registration right. Demand registration rights give an investor the right to force a company to register its shares with the SEC. A demand registration right gives an investor control over the timing of a registration and in effect means that the investor can force the company to go public. See chapter 4, section 21 – Registration Rights.

Dilution — see Economic dilution, Price-based dilution and Dilution of ownership.

Dilution of ownership — the reduction in the ownership percentage of current investors, founders and employees caused by the issuance of new shares to new investors.

Dividends — a share of profits paid by a company to its shareholders. Dividends can be paid in cash or in shares.

Down round — a financing round in which the valuation of the company is lower than the value determined by investors in an earlier round.

Drag-along rights — a right that enables a shareholder to force the other shareholders to sell their shares of the company. See chapter 4, section 28 – Drag-Along Right.

Due diligence — an investigation of a company aimed at assessing the viability of a potential investment and the accuracy of the information provided by the company. This investigation usually focuses on the legal, financial, tax and commercial position of the company.

Dynamic equity split — the concept that everyone involved in the early-stage phase of a start-up receives rewards (that can be converted into equity) for their contribution, based on an agreed calculation method.

Early stage — the early phase of a company's life. This term is used to indicate the phase after the seed (formation) stage but before the phase in which the company starts generating revenues.

Employee Stock Option Plan (ESOP) or (Restricted) Stock Ownership Plan — a plan established by a company to let certain employees benefit strongly from the increase in value of the company. Under an ESOP, certain employees have a right to buy shares in the company at a predetermined price (exercise price) within a specified period of time (exercise period). Under a (Restricted) Stock Ownership Plan, employees are not granted options, but buy shares at once. ESOPs and (Restricted) Stock Ownership Plans offer companies a way to employ (and retain) high-quality people at relatively low salaries. See chapter 4, section 30 – Employee Pool.

Equity — Equity represents ownership in a company and is usually represented by common shares and preferred shares. Equity is equal to assets less liabilities.

ESOP — see Employee Stock Option Plan.

Founder — a person who participates in the creation of a company.

Full ratchet protection — a type of anti-dilution protection. If new preferred shares are issued to investor B at a (per share) price that is lower than the price investor A paid in an earlier round, the effect of the full ratchet is that the per share price of investor A is adjusted downward to the price paid by investor B. Usually, as a result of the implementation of a full ratchet, the company management and employees who own common shares suffer significant dilution. See chapter 4, section 14 – Anti-Dilution.

Fully diluted basis — a methodology for calculating per share ratios. Under this methodology, the denominator is equal to the total number of shares issued by the company, whereby it is assumed that all common share equivalents (such as convertible notes, convertible preferred shares, options, warrants, etc.) have been converted into common shares.

Initial public offering (IPO) — a company's first sale of shares to the public also referred to as going public. An IPO is one of the ways in which a company can raise additional capital for further growth.

Internal rate of return (IRR) — the interest rate at which a certain amount of capital today would have to be invested in order to grow to a specific value at a specific time in the future.

IPO — see Initial public offering.

IRR — see Internal Rate of Return.

Issuer — the company issuing securities.

Later stage — the later phase of a company's life. In this phase, the company has proven its concept, achieved significant revenues and is approaching cash flow break-even or positive net income. A later stage company is typically about six to twelve months away from a liquidity event such as an IPO or strategic take-over.

Lead investor — The firm or individual that organises a round of financing and usually contributes the largest amount of capital to the deal.

Liquidation — The selling of all the assets of a company and the use of the cash proceeds of the sale to pay off creditors prior to the complete cessation of operations.

Liquidation preference — the right of an investor to priority in receiving the proceeds from the sale or liquidation of a company. This right is usually attached to the preferred shares and gives the holders of such shares a position that is senior or ahead of the holders of common shares or junior preferred shares if the company is sold or liquidated.

Liquidity event — an event that allows an investor to realise a gain or loss on his investment. Examples of liquidity events include Initial Public Offerings (IPOs), trade sales, buy-outs and take-overs.

Lock-up agreement — an agreement not to sell or transfer shares in a company for a specific period. Underwriters, for example, require lock-up agreements in most IPOs. In such cases, they will usually require the largest shareholders and directors of the company to agree to a lock-up period of six months following the IPO.

Narrow-based weighted average anti-dilution — a system used in connection with anti-dilution protection. A narrow-based weighted average protection adjusts downward the price per share of the preferred stock of investor A due to the issuance of new preferred shares to a new investor B at a price lower than the price investor A originally paid. Investor A's preferred shares are re-priced to a weighted average of investor A's price and investor B's price. If a narrow-based weighted average system is used, the denominator of the formula for determining the new weighted average price contains only a total number of outstanding shares (as opposed to the number shares on a fully diluted basis). This number can vary from all pre-money outstanding shares (on a non-converted and non-diluted basis) to only the preferred shares issued in the previous round. The narrower the base, the larger the effect of the new price and the more favourable the clause is to the protected investors. See chapter 4, section 14 – Anti-Dilution.

Non-compete — an agreement often signed by key employees and other persons (such as management) who are key to the success of a company pursuant to which such persons agree not to work for competitor companies or form a new competitor company within a certain time period after termination of their employment with the company.

Non-cumulative dividends — dividends that do not cumulate. In other words, if the cash flow of the company is insufficient to make payment of dividend possible at a certain point in time, the owners of the shares entitled to non-cumulative dividends will not receive the dividend owed for the time period in question (also not at a later stage) and will have to wait until another set of dividends is declared.

Non-solicitation — an agreement often signed by employees and management that prohibits such persons, once they have left the company, from soliciting the customers and employees of the company.

Non-disclosure agreement — an agreement often signed by key employees and management that is aimed at protecting the company against improper disclosure or use of the company-sensitive information and materials that are not known to the general public.

Pay-to-play — a clause that is aimed at punishing investors who do not participate on a pro rata basis in a financing round, by cancelling some or all of their preferential rights. The most onerous version of pay-to-play is automatic conversion to common shares, which in essence ends any preferential rights of an investor, such as the right to influence important management decisions.

Pari passu — a legal term that means in equal proportion. It usually refers to the equal treatment of two or more parties in an agreement.

Participating dividends — the right of holders of certain preferred shares to receive their preferred dividends <u>and</u> share (with the common shareholders) in the dividends available for distribution after the preferred dividend has been paid. See chapter 4, section 10 – Dividends.

Participating preferred share — a preferred share that is entitled to participating dividends. A participating preferred share can in effect be split into two parts: a preferred share part and common share part. The preferred share part entitles the owner to receive a predetermined cash dividend. The common share part represents additional continued ownership in the company.

Piggyback right — the right of an investor to follow in the process to have shares registered. In the case of piggyback rights, this process is initiated and controlled by others. Consequently, the investor cannot force the company to go public. See chapter 4, section 21 – Registration Rights.

Post-money valuation — the valuation of a company immediately after an investment in the company. If, for example, an investor invests €2 million in a company valued at €1 million pre-money (before the investment was made), the post-money valuation will be €3 million.

Preference — a preferred position, or seniority. In venture capital transactions investors usually have preference with respect to dividends and proceeds from a liquidity event, for example.

Preferred share — a type of share to which certain special rights are attached that are not attached to common shares. These special rights may include preferred dividends, anti-dilution protection, voting rights, drag-along rights, tag-along rights, liquidity preference, rights of first refusal, etc. A venture capital investor will normally only subscribe to preferred shares.

Pre-money valuation — the valuation of a company immediately before an investment in the company.

Private equity — equity investments in non-public companies.

Private placement — the sale of securities directly to a limited number of investors.

Prospectus — a formal written offer to sell securities that sets forth a plan for a (proposed) business opportunity and that gives sufficient detail about such opportunity for a prospective investor to make a decision.

Qualified IPO (or Qualified Offering) — a public offering of securities that meets certain predetermined criteria, such as a minimum per share price and minimum proceeds to the company.

Redemption rights — the right of an investor to force the company to repurchase the investors' preferred shares.
Registration — the process whereby shares of a company are registered with the relevant authorities in preparation for a sale of the shares to the public.
Registration rights — the rights of an investor in a company regarding the registration of the company's shares for sale to the public. Examples of registration rights are piggyback rights and demand rights. See chapter 4, section 21 – Registration Rights.
Right of first refusal — a right to match any offer made for shares held by a shareholder, under the same terms and conditions, and thus to pre-empt any other buyers. See chapter 4, section 26 – Rights of First Refusal.
Round — an event whereby financing is provided to a company by one or more investors.
Security — a document that indicates that the holder owns a portion of a company's equity or debt, or has the right to purchase or sell such portion. Shares, notes, bonds and options are examples of securities.
Seed round — the first financing round after incorporation of the Company. Funds are provided by seed venture capitalists, angels (high-net-worth individuals) or friends and family to the founders of a start-up company. The amount raised with a seed round usually does not exceed 2 million euros.
Seniority — higher priority.
Series A preferred shares — preferred shares issued by a company in exchange for capital from investors in the Series A round of financing.
Series A round — the first significant financing round in which one or more venture capitalist(s) become(s) involved in a fast-growing company that was previously financed by founders, seed venture capitalists and/or angels. Usually, a Series A round raises from two to ten million euros.
Series B round — the financing round following the Series A round in which additional funds are provided to the company. Subsequent rounds are called C, D, and so on.
Stock — a share of ownership in a company.
Stock Appreciation Rights (SARs) — rights, usually granted to employees, to receive a bonus equal to the appreciation in the company's shares over a specified period.
Stock option — a right to purchase or sell a share at a specific price within a specific period.

Subordinated debt — a loan over which a senior loan takes priority. In the event of a liquidation of the company, subordinated debt-holders receive payment only after senior debt is paid in full. Also known as junior debt.

Syndicate — a group of investors that agree to provide capital to a company under the same terms. The term syndicate can also refer to a group of (investment) banks that agree to participate in, for example, the sale of stock to the public as part of an IPO.

Tag-along right — the right of an investor to include his shares in any sale by another shareholder at the same price and under the same terms and conditions which apply to such other shareholder. Also referred to as Co-sale right. See chapter 4, section 27 – Co-Sale Right.

Term sheet — a document summarising the basic terms and conditions under which investors are prepared to make a potential investment in a company.

Underwriter — an investment bank that commits to the successful distribution of a public issue, failing which the bank would take the securities being offered into its own books.

Value inflection point — an event or series of events that results in a significant change in the value of a company. An inflection point can be considered a turning point after which a dramatic change, with either positive or negative results, is expected to result.

Venture capital — a segment of the private equity industry, which focuses on investing in new companies with a high growth-rate.

Voluntary conversion — the right of an investor to convert his preferred shares into common shares.

Voting right — the right of a shareholder to vote on certain matters affecting the company.

Warrant — a right to buy a specified number of shares at a fixed exercise price by exercising such right prior to a specified expiration date. A warrant is a long-term option, usually valid for several years or indefinitely. See chapter 4, section 6 – Warrant Coverage.

Weighted average protection — a type of anti-dilution protection. If new preferred shares are issued to investor B at a (per share) price which is lower than the price investor A paid in an earlier round, the effect of the weighted average protection is that the per share price of investor A is adjusted downward to a weighted average of the price paid by investor A and the price paid by investor B. For the new price the weighting factor is the number of shares issued in the dilutive financing round. For the old price, the factor is either (i) the total number of common shares outstanding prior to the dilutive financing round on an as-if converted and fully diluted basis (broad based weighted average) or (ii) any number of shares outstanding prior to the dilutive financing round less than the number under (i) (narrow based weighted average). See chapter 4, section 14 – Anti-Dilution.

Zone of misalignment — the range of exit values were the interests of the holders of common shares and preferred shares are misaligned due to the effects of the liquidation preference.

ANNEX 4:
IRR ANALYSIS: YEARS INVESTED VS. RETURN MULTIPLE

Return Multiple	1.5x	2.0x	3.0x	4.0x	5.0x	6.0x	7.0x	8.0x	9.0x	10.0x
Years Invested										
2	22%	41%	73%	100%	124%	145%	165%	183%	200%	216%
3	14%	26%	44%	59%	71%	82%	91%	100%	108%	115%
4	11%	19%	32%	41%	50%	57%	63%	68%	73%	78%
5	8%	15%	25%	32%	38%	43%	48%	52%	55%	58%
6	7%	12%	20%	26%	31%	35%	38%	41%	44%	47%
7	6%	10%	17%	22%	26%	29%	32%	35%	37%	39%
8	5%	9%	15%	19%	22%	25%	28%	30%	32%	33%
9	5%	8%	13%	17%	20%	22%	24%	26%	28%	29%
10	4%	7%	12%	15%	17%	20%	21%	23%	25%	26%

Example

Multiple	Years	IRR	Invested	Returned
4.0x	5.00	32%	01-01-17	31-12-21
			€(100.00)	€400.00

Grayed IRR Cells = IRR that is at or above the desired IRR.

NOTES

TERMS EXPLAINED

TERMS EXPLAINED

Made in the USA
Columbia, SC
05 January 2024